The New Local Government Series

No. 5

THE
LOCAL GOVERNMENT SYSTEM

The New Local Government Series

Series Editor: Professor Peter G. Richards

6 THE FINANCE OF LOCAL GOVERNMENT
by N. P. Hepworth

8 TOWN AND COUNTRY PLANNING IN BRITAIN
by J. B. Cullingworth

12 DEMOCRATIC THEORY AND LOCAL GOVERNMENT
by Dilys M. Hill

13 THE LOCAL GOVERNMENT ACT 1972: PROBLEMS OF
IMPLEMENTATION
by Peter G. Richards

14 THE PROCESS OF LOCAL GOVERNMENT REFORM 1966–1974
by Bruce Wood

15 LOCAL GOVERNMENT AND EDUCATION
by D. E. Regan

16 THE LOCAL GOVERNMENT SERVICE
IN ENGLAND AND WALES
by K. P. Poole

17 A HISTORY OF LOCAL GOVERNMENT IN THE
TWENTIETH CENTURY
by Bryan Keith-Lucas and Peter G. Richards

18 LOCAL GOVERNMENT IN BRITAIN AND FRANCE
Problems and Prospects
Edited by Jacques Lagroye and Vincent Wright

19 ORGANISATION THEORY AND LOCAL GOVERNMENT
by Robert J. Haynes

20 POWER AND PARTY IN AN ENGLISH CITY
An Account of Single-Party Rule
by David G. Green

21 ECONOMIC POLICY-MAKING BY LOCAL AUTHORITIES
IN BRITAIN AND WESTERN GERMANY
by Nevil Johnson and Allan Cochrane

22 BRITISH DOGMATISM AND FRENCH PRAGMATISM
Central–Local Policy-Making in the Welfare State
by Douglas E. Ashford

23 LOCAL GOVERNMENT IN BRITAIN SINCE REORGANISATION
by Alan Alexander

THE
LOCAL GOVERNMENT
SYSTEM

BY

PETER G. RICHARDS

Professor of British Government
University of Southampton

London
GEORGE ALLEN & UNWIN
Boston   Sydney

George Allen & Unwin (Publishers) Ltd,
40 Museum Street, London WC1A 1LU, UK

George Allen & Unwin (Publishers) Ltd,
Park Lane, Hemel Hempstead, Herts HP2 4TE, UK

Allen & Unwin, Inc.,
9 Winchester Terrace, Winchester, Mass. 01890, USA

George Allen & Unwin Australia Pty Ltd,
8 Napier Street, North Sydney, NSW 2060, Australia

The Local Government System is the successor-volume to
The Reformed Local Government System, first published in this series in 1973
First published in 1983

British Library Cataloguing in Publication Data

Richards, Peter G.
   The local government system. – (The New local government series; no. 5)
1. Local government – England
I. Title   II. Series
352.042   JS31111
ISBN 0-04-352104-5
ISBN 0-04-352105-3 Pbk

Library of Congress Cataloging in Publication Data

Richards, Peter G.
   The local government system.
"Successor-volume to The reformed local government system" – T.p. verso.
Bibliography: p.
Includes index.
1. Local government – Great Britain.
I. Richards, Peter G. The reformed local government system.   II. Title.
JS3095 1983   352.042   82-11481
ISBN 0-04-352104-5
ISBN 0-04-352105-3 (pbk.)

Set in 10 on 11 pt Times by
Computape (Pickering) Ltd., North Yorkshire
Printed in Great Britain by
Biddles Ltd, Guildford, Surrey

PREFACE

The present system of local government in England and Wales is based on the Local Government Act 1972. This Act came into force on 1 April 1974 in an atmosphere of some optimism and expectation for the future. At the time horizons were still expanding. It was believed that local authorities could and would make a growing contribution to improving the quality of life for all citizens. Now the outlook has wholly changed. Cuts in public expenditure require cuts in the standards of services. Without question, local government is in decline.

My previous introductory volume to the Allen & Unwin local government series was first published in 1973. Its title *The Reformed Local Government System* reflected the contemporary spirit of movement and progress. Today a rather different approach is needed. This book retains some of the historical and descriptive material from the 1973 volume, but the analytical commentary is new.

The book is intended for use by students, by the younger local government officers, by councillors and by all those interested in local public affairs. Yet the intention is not simply to inform. I believe that local government is a valuable support for the whole democratic process, that damage to local government is a wound to our tradition of a free society. Local government, if it is to be real, implies local differences. Certainly our system is too centralised for these variations to be major. Nevertheless, they relate to local opinion that is not always uniform. Moves towards variation should be respected and not always suppressed. So the book not only describes our local institutions; it also attempts to make a case in their favour.

As ever, I am grateful to the secretarial staff of the Politics Department for help with the typing. And my wife tries to ensure that clarity of expression is well maintained.

PETER G. RICHARDS

University of Southampton
December 1981

CONTENTS

PREFACE   *page*   7

1   *Historical Introduction*   11

     Traditional Units and their Decline
     Nineteenth-Century Reform
     Proposals for Change 1945–72

2   *The Basis of the System*   36

     Types of Local Authority
     County – District Relationships
     The Committee System
     Standing Orders
     The Associations of Local Authorities

3   *Functions*   59

     The Acquisition of Powers
     Growth of Services
     The Allocation of Duties

4   *Politics and Personnel*   73

     The Impact of Politics
     Councillors
     Leaders, Chairmen and Mayors
     Officers

5   *Finance*   92

     A System in Decay
     Rating
     Government Grants
     Capital Expenditure
     Rates – Inadequate and Unfair?

6   *Central Control*   115

     The Constitutional Basis
     Supervision by Whitehall
     District Audit
     Central–Local Relations

7 *The Quest for Efficiency*   *page* 139
       Personnel Management
       Co-ordination of Policy and Administration
       Modern Techniques of Management

8 *Local Government and Society*   159
       The Pattern of Pressures
       Complaints Machinery
       Public Participation and Accountability
       The Case for Local Government

APPENDIX A   Size of Local Authorities   177

APPENDIX B   Allocation of Main Functions   180

FURTHER READING   184

INDEX   187

Chapter 1

HISTORICAL INTRODUCTION

The present system of local government in England and Wales cannot be fully appreciated without reference to the past. Yet the history of local government is a vast subject on its own – witness the magnificent works of Sidney and Beatrice Webb. In an introductory book the historical element must be a mere sketch. This chapter is a sketch of the development of local government, but one that concentrates on the interrelationship of local administrative areas, local services and local resources. It also tries to link the growth of local services with the dominant trends in political thought at least since 1834. How people react to social problems depends on what they feel to be morally right: the moral drive behind much of local government is one aspect too often overlooked.

TRADITIONAL UNITS AND THEIR DECLINE

The three traditional units of local government in England and Wales have been the county, the parish and the borough. Each has had its own functions which were exercised with a large degree of independence, although the county justices had supervisory powers over parish officers. However, the sense of separateness was so strong that the idea of a *local government system* with major and minor local authorities with interlocking responsibilities did not emerge clearly until the latter part of the nineteenth century. By modern standards, the local units of government also suffered little central control. Central interference varied with the political situation of the time – the later Stuart kings, in particular, tried to ensure that local positions of influence were held by their supporters – but local institutions were left to deal with local problems in the way they thought best. Since national grants were unknown until the 1840s, the scale of county, parish and borough activity was minimal. Indeed, much effort was expended in the eighteenth century on the promotion of new local bodies to carry out tasks which the traditional authorities were unable or unwilling to undertake.

The county has its origins in feudal times when it was the territory granted by the king to an earl in return for acceptance of feudal obligations. After the feudal period justices of the peace chosen through the king's representative, the Lord Lieutenant, became responsible for county government. Initially the justices were essentially concerned with the maintenance of law and order. Thus their functions were primarily judicial. However, they had some administrative responsibilities, mainly for prisons and bridges, and they had to settle disputes arising out of the actions of parish officers. Visiting justices made irregular visits to parishes to inspect their poor law accounts.

Boroughs were based on charters granted at different times by the monarchy. These charters were valuable because they gave a small town the right to have its own justices and, therefore, to have its own court: this saved much difficulty and expense since disputes could be settled locally and without the need for a possibly unpleasant journey to the quarter sessions. Charters also gave the right to hold markets and so assisted trade and prosperity. They also provided for separate parliamentary representation, but this was commonly regarded as a mixed blessing because of the cost and danger of travel to Westminster. Often borough charters were granted by the king in the expectation of being able to control the nominations to the House of Commons made by the borough. The borough corporations themselves were usually renewed through a process of self-co-option.

The parish was originally the smallest unit of church organisation. It gradually acquired non-ecclesiastical functions, starting with highways in the sixteenth century and the care of the poor in 1601. Frequently the word 'vestry' was used instead of parish because meetings to discuss parish business were held in the church vestry. The names 'open vestry' and 'closed vestry' described how far parish business was open to all parishioners; in a closed vestry decisions would be taken by the local elite – the people who were the largest ratepayers in the parish. Whether any particular vestry was open or closed generally depended on local convention rather than law.

For the common people the parish became the most important local unit of government as it had the greatest effect on their lives. The ancient liability that highways should be repaired 'by the inhabitants at large' was enforced through the parish. By the Statute of Highways 1555 each parish had to appoint two surveyors responsible for the repair of roads in the parish, and the inhabitants were required to devote four days' labour to this work of maintenance. The more wealthy members of the community chose to pay a highway rate instead of doing the work themselves and the money collected was used to pay the poor for working on the roads. The administrative duties of the parish became truly burdensome after 1601 when it was made responsible for the relief of the poor. The

Elizabethan poor law required each parish to appoint an overseer who would impose a rate on the local inhabitants to raise money for the purchase of materials on which the poor could be put to work. The theory was that the goods made would be sold and the revenue could then be distributed to relieve poverty. Thus the poor would be helped, but they would also have to work to help themselves. The theory was commendable, but in practice, the idea could not work. The administration required was too complex for an unpaid parish officer to carry out: even where working materials were provided, paupers were often so old, ill, or unskilled, or living in such bad conditions that useful work could not be done. The scheme collapsed and was replaced by the gratuitous distribution of relief financed by a parish rate. Especially in times of bad trade the cost of the poor law was heavy and often caused dispute within a parish.

Each parish carried out its duties through four types of unpaid officer – the overseer of the poor, the surveyor, the constable and the churchwarden. The duties of the first two have already been described. The constable was responsible for keeping the peace and took offenders before the magistrates. The churchwarden was responsible for the maintenance of the fabric of the parish church and, if necessary, collected a rate from the parish to pay for this to be done. Often the necessary funds were subscribed by the wealthy and church rates were rarely required. Necessarily they provoked opposition and indignation from nonconformists who did not attend the parish church. In 1837 the Braintree vestry refused to agree to a church rate and when the churchwarden tried to collect the money without authority his action was successfully challenged in the courts. In 1868 the Gladstone Liberal government abolished church rates and cut another link between ecclesiastical and civil administration.

The parish officers were appointed at the vestry meeting. Since the work was substantial in amount and sometimes unpleasant, it was not always easy to find persons willing to serve. However, the system worked because of a general feeling that good citizens should accept a share of social responsibility. Often the jobs were passed round at the end of a year's duty. Some parishes had an understanding that a parish officer could nominate his successor. The overseer had the heaviest task and in some places a payment was made to him for his trouble; this might be done quite unofficially by means of private donations from the well-to-do inhabitants. Yet the whole system depended on part-time service and goodwill. It was quite unable to accept any wider responsibilities, so when demands came forward for extra and improved local administration the parish was bypassed. More efficient and more complex social provision required better qualified, paid and full-time staff which, in turn, required a larger unit of organisation than the parish. Equally, the county and the borough were ill-placed to obtain extra duties, especially those involving the expenditure of public money. They were not representative bodies and not responsible to the public. So there were obvious grounds for refusing them any further taxing powers. In addition, some borough corporations and, indeed, some magistrates in urban areas were widely accused of corruption – of using official positions to secure personal gain. In the pre-railway age the larger counties were also regarded as too large a unit to be convenient for local administration.

Since the parish, the county and the borough were unsuitable to deal with the social problems arising from the growth of trade, the industrial revolution and the growth of population, new local government institutions were created. The three most important were the turnpike trusts, the Improvement Commissioners and the poor law unions.

The turnpikes were urgently needed to improve the state of the roads. In the eighteenth century there was a dramatic increase in the amount of road transport largely because of more trade but also because people started to travel more for pleasure or for health reasons. To place responsibility for maintaining roads on the parish was both inefficient and unfair. The largest parishes in terms of area were normally those in sparsely populated countryside, while the smaller parishes were in the more thickly populated districts. There was no correlation between the resources of a parish in terms of money or labour and the extent of its highway responsibilities: a parish with a tiny population could have a long stretch of a road running through it which linked major towns. Turnpike trusts were established by Acts of Parliament to charge tolls on travellers for using a road and the proceeds of the tolls could meet the cost of repairing the roads. Today many old toll houses can still be seen situated by the side of main roads.

The growth of towns aggravated many problems of urban living. As in the countryside there was a greater need to maintain roads, but there was also a need for drainage and for the effective maintenance of law and order, particularly the prevention of robbery. Many of the new industrial towns had no municipal corporation: elsewhere the corporations were in the hands of a limited clique and were not respected by the greater part of the citizens. So throughout the country bodies of Improvement Commissions were established by locally sponsored Acts of Parliament. The Commissioners were nominated in the local Act and renewed by co-option, but by the early days of the nineteenth century the principle of ratepayer election was introduced. Their powers varied and were defined in each local Act. In towns adjacent to rivers or the sea they often provided docking facilities and were known as Harbour and Improvement Commissioners. In general, they were responsible for lighting, paving and draining streets and for providing a watch – an embryonic police force.

Undoubtedly, the most expensive and most contentious branch of local administration was poor relief. During the eighteenth century the parish was already losing control of this function. Various Acts strengthened the power of the justices to supervise the distribution of relief. In 1795 the magistrates of Speenhamland drew up a scale of payment which related the amount of relief payable to the size of a pauper's family and to the price of bread; this Speenhamland scale was widely adopted by justices and overseers. Parliament also permitted parishes to work together in dealing with the poor. An Act of 1723 allowed parishes to join together and form unions which could build workhouses where the poor could live and work. This power was not widely used but another Act of 1782 authorised parishes to join together in unions so they could appoint paid officers to carry out the distribution of relief. These poor law unions were controlled by Guardians, originally appointed by the justices, but subsequently elected by ratepayers.

Two features dominated the law of local administration – it was both local and permissive. Only some main traffic routes were cared for by turnpikes; others were covered partially or not at all. Only some parishes agreed to join poor law unions. The powers of Improvement Commissioners varied as did their relationship, if any, with the local municipal corporation. Until late in the nineteenth century nothing existed that could be described as a coherent system of local services – instead there was a chaos of institutions, areas and rates.

NINETEENTH-CENTURY REFORM

The political upheaval which produced the 1832 Reform Bill had an immediate impact on local administration. The first major change concerned the poor law. In 1832 a Poor Law Commission was appointed to report on the working of the existing arrangements and the Commission sent out investigators to examine conditions in about 300 parishes. These investigators may be considered as the forerunners of the present-day inspectorate. The Commission's report portrayed a situation of confusion, incompetence and waste. The Poor Law Amendment Act 1834, based on the Commission's recommendations, provided a new and uniform basis for poor relief.

A central body in London, the Poor Law Commission, was to supervise the whole system – the start of central control over the detailed administration of local services. The central body united parishes into convenient areas for poor law purposes and in so doing ignored other traditional divisions. Thus many unions overlapped county boundaries. The poor law unions were also *ad hoc* bodies, that is, they were formed to carry out a particular service. This was not a new idea in 1834 for turnpikes had then existed for many years, but the poor law unions were the first example of a pattern of *ad hoc* authorities covering the whole country; now there are many examples of this kind, water and health authorities and the area organisations of public corporations. The Poor Law Commission laid down strict rules covering the distribution of relief. The unions were to build workhouses and the distribution of relief other than to the inmates of the workhouse was banned: the regime in the workhouse was to be spartan to deter applications for admission. Local Boards of Guardians were elected by the ratepayers to run the workhouses, subject to national control.

The other major reform of the 1830s applied to the municipal corporations. Once more a commission of inquiry was appointed and Assistant Commissioners were sent out to examine how the corporations were conducted. Again the report was damning. Some corporations were so decayed as to be virtually non-existent; many did nothing of value for the local inhabitants; some were corrupt. The Municipal Corporations Act 1835 gave the boroughs a new constitution and insisted on proper financial management. Borough councillors were to be elected by the ratepayers and the House of Lords required that a quarter of the council should consist of aldermen elected by the councillors. All borough revenues were to be paid into a single fund to be used for the benefit of the inhabitants. The administration of justice was divorced from the administration of services and the borough justices were separated from the borough council. But in contrast to the Poor Law Amendment Act, the amount of central control was negligible. The major task of the borough was the maintenance of law and order and the 1835 Act decreed that a quarterly report from the local Watch Committee be submitted to the Home Secretary. A borough could also make by-laws for the good rule and government of its area which were subject to approval of the Privy Council. The Treasury was empowered to stop the sale and long leases of corporation-owned land. Yet the total effect of these controls was small. The 1835 Act did nothing to change the area of boroughs. It was applied to 178 towns. Other places which claimed borough status were ignored and the corporations deprived of recognition faded away.

The City of London also managed to avoid coming under these provisions: many attempts in the following fifty years to reform London government were frustrated by the powerful financial interests of the City.

These two Acts demonstrate a remarkable difference of approach. The poor law reform was based on central control, uniformity, rationalisation of areas and the *ad hoc* principle. The Municipal Corporations Act emphasised the authority of local representatives subject to a minimum of central direction, maintained existing areas and created an organisation capable of dealing with a wide range of services. All these contrasts recur in the subsequent history of local government. Indeed, they form the basis of much of the recent discussion about the shape of future local government reform.

In the 1840s public attention was concentrated on the question of health. This concern was largely stimulated by Edwin Chadwick, Secretary of the Poor Law Commissioners, who was convinced that disease was the main cause of poverty, and that the best way to help the poor was to remove the causes of sickness. Reports of official inquiries, heavily influenced by Chadwick, slowly created public willingness for government action. The two major reports on the Sanitary Condition of the Labouring Population (1842) and the State of Large Towns (1845) revealed almost unbelievable conditions of filth, squalor and a lack of drainage and pure water supplies. The Public Health Act 1848 authorised the establishment of local Boards of Health to provide water supply and drainage, either where the inhabitants requested it or where the death rate exceeded 23 per 1,000. Municipal Corporations became the Boards of Health for their own areas. The work of the local Boards was to be supervised by a Central Board of Health. Earlier, in 1846, the Poor Law Guardians had been given limited powers to deal with insanitary nuisances in rural areas.

The public health legislation to a large extent followed the model of the poor law reform. However, there were differences, which grew larger as time passed. The element of central control was present and more *ad hoc* bodies were created. However, more scope was allowed for local initiative and the Central Board of Health never achieved the dominance of the Poor Law Commission. The Central Board was reorganised in 1854 and dissolved in 1858, its functions being divided between the Privy Council and the Home Office. (The original Poor Law Commission had been displaced in 1847 by a minister, the President of the Poor Law Board, who was directly answerable to Parliament: but the central direction of poor relief remained firm.) The opposition to central direction on health questions was due to the disappearance of epidemics and the dislike of spending large sums of money that had to be raised by local taxation. Yet even when the *laissez-faire* reaction swept away the Central Board of Health in 1858 there remained 670 local Boards of Health which continued to promote more civilised conditions in urban areas.

After a decade of inaction at national level, the Royal Sanitary Commission was appointed in 1868. Its report in 1871 set out the requirements 'of what is necessary for a civilised social life' which included a pure water supply, sewage, burial arrangements and the inspection of food. A new government department, the Local Government Board, was created in 1871 to deal with these matters. In 1872 the whole country was divided up into urban and rural sanitary districts, the urban authorities being given wider powers. The urban authorities were boroughs, Improvement Commissioners and local Boards of Health: Poor Law Guardians became sanitary authorities for the parts of their union not included in the above. Thus while the Guardians combined both town and country for poor law purposes, they dealt with public health matters solely in the countryside. This separation of urban and rural areas was a reversal of one of the principles of the 1834 poor law reform and created the basis of the later distinction between urban and rural districts.

At this period the question of highway maintenance became acute as the turnpike trust system was breaking down. The new steam railways provided an alternative means of transport and adversely affected the revenues of the turnpikes, so reducing their ability to keep roads in good repair. There was also increased public opposition to the payment of tolls. In South Wales rioters destroyed turnpike gates. Consequently Parliament refused to renew the powers of the turnpike trusts when they lapsed and the disturnpiked roads reverted to the care of the parish. Even in the eighteenth century it had been widely accepted that the parish was not competent to maintain the roads and the obvious need was for the creation of a highway authority based on a larger unit than the parish. The county was unacceptable since the county justices were not elected. The alternative was to form unions of parishes on the model of the poor law. In 1862 the county justices were given powers to create such unions, but often these were based on the areas of the justices' petty sessional districts, not on the areas of the poor law unions. This added substantially to the confusion of local administration in rural areas. Highway districts were highly unpopular. They imposed a financial obligation upon the parish rate which had no connection with the extent of the traditional liability of the parish to maintain its own roads. Parishes suffered if small in area with substantial population; parishes gained if large in area with a small population. In some cases the gains and losses were heavy. Many large villages managed to opt out of a highway district by adopting the Public Health Act 1848 and forming their own local Board of Health which entitled them to separate highway powers. In 1863 this trick was stopped by an Act which stipulated that only parishes with a population of at least 3,000 could adopt the Public Health Act. Meanwhile some very small pre-1974 urban districts owed their existence to the scramble to avoid inclusion in a highway union. The resistance to highway unions was so acute that in some areas they were never formed. In other places they were allowed to decay and responsibility for the roads again fell back on the parish. Elsewhere the areas were rationalised and made to conform with the poor law unions, yet this was often difficult because the poor law unions frequently overlapped county boundaries.

Today many local authority areas are anomalous: in the nineteenth century they were fantastic. Over a thousand parishes included one or more parcels of land completely detached from the main body of the parish; in the west of England the separated parts were occasionally situated in a different county. This jigsaw necessarily complicated local administration. The parish of Threapwood in the Wrexham poor law union was partly in Cheshire and partly in Denbighshire and so was part in England and part in Wales. A woman in the village, a pauper, went mad and had to be sent to an asylum. In England the charge for maintaining a pauper lunatic was 14s a week, in Wales it was only 8s a week. The question arose whether the woman was domiciled in the English or the Welsh sector of the village. The Clerk of the Wrexham Union discovered that the house where the woman was born was astride the county boundary. However, he was able to establish that the woman was born in the Welsh piece of the house and so saved his authority 6s a week. This cameo is drawn from evidence presented to the Select Committee on Parish, Union and County Boundaries which reported in 1873. Gradually parish boundaries were rationalised, but the process was slow.

Parish boundaries achieved greater importance because of both roads and education. In 1870 Gladstone's first Liberal government imposed on the parish the responsibility of providing a school if an adequate one had not been provided by voluntary agencies – that is, the churches. School attendance became compulsory in 1876 and free in 1891. The eccentric boundaries had effects which appeared inequitable. The main part of a parish could have a satisfactory church school but no provision for children in a detached piece some distance off; the whole parish was required to contribute to the provision of a school for the detached part. Even in 1870 the parish was obviously too small a unit to be a satisfactory education authority. However, since many parishes already had schools it was impossible to create school unions in which the cost could be pooled: such an arrangement would have aroused even more antagonism than the highway unions.

Over the years various pressures developed which made a democratic reform of county government long overdue. Agricultural labourers gained the parliamentary franchise through the third Reform Bill 1884. The anomaly that boroughs, but not counties, enjoyed representative government had existed for half a century. The administrative duties of the county justice had grown steadily and so had the size of the county rate demand. In particular, the village constable was replaced by the county police force in 1856. It became clear that further services, notably highways, ought to be made a county responsibility in order to achieve better and more uniform standards of repair and to spread the cost over a wider area. Finally, administration in the London area was seriously in need of reform. London had grown far beyond the area of the City, which had successfully avoided all attempts to modernise its constitution. Many important services were provided by the Metropolitan Board of Works established in 1855 which was based on a system of indirect election through a pattern of district boards. The Metropolitan Board had been responsible for substantial redevelopment in the West End but had become corrupt. Beyond question, London needed unified and democratic local government. These pressures, combined with the influence of Joseph Chamberlain and the Liberal Unionists within Lord Salisbury's Conservative government, succeeded in making a major reform. The Local Government Act 1888 remained the foundation of our present system of local government – outside London – until the coming into force of the Local Government Act 1972.

The 1888 Act had three major aspects. It created a new system of county councils elected on a ratepayer franchise; it defined the relationship between the county councils and the boroughs; it reorganised the financial relations between central and local government. When originally introduced the Bill had a further section covering the reform of small authorities within the county, but this had to be dropped for lack of parliamentary time. After a delay of six years this part of the reform was enacted in 1894.

The new county councils did not correspond entirely with the historic counties. Some were divided for administrative convenience because of the size of the county, for example, Yorkshire, or its shape, for example, Sussex. To a great extent these divisions often represented existing practice in that the county magistrates had met in separate centres and had levied separate rates. The bisection of Suffolk was based on acceptance of current arrangements. The problem of the metropolis was solved by carving a new county, the London County Council, out of Middlesex, Surrey and Kent, the LCC boundaries being based on those of the superseded Metropolitan Board of Works. Two years after the Act was passed the Isle of Wight was also made a separate county. Thus the trisection of Yorkshire and Lincolnshire, the division of Cambridgeshire, Northamptonshire, Hampshire, Suffolk and Sussex, together with the new county of London created a total of sixty-two county councils out of the fifty-two geographical counties

Initially the powers given to the counties were limited. Their major task was to care for those roads designated as county roads. A joint committee was formed with the county justices to supervise the county police force. They also inherited from the county justices an assortment of administrative duties, many relating to the issue of licences for various purposes. In subsequent years the counties acquired a wide range of functions. Indeed, the history of local government in the twentieth century can be largely summarised by listing the extensions to county responsibilities.

Much parliamentary time was consumed by the representatives of boroughs fighting for their independence from the new county councils. As originally drafted the Bill excluded only the very largest towns with a population of 150,000 from the aegis of the counties. This implied that all other boroughs would be subordinate to the county councils and would have to pay the county rate. Previously boroughs with their own quarter sessions had been exempt from the county rate because the administrative duties of the county justices had been carried out by their own borough bench. Under pressure from borough MPs the size of boroughs with county power – that is, county boroughs – was reduced to 50,000 population, and four smaller boroughs, Burton-on-Trent, Canterbury, Chester and Worcester, were also admitted to the select band.

The financial sections of the 1888 Act were an attempt to secure some order and principle for methods of giving monetary aid to local authorities. At various dates since the Chadwick era Exchequer grants had been given in respect of education, police, highways, criminal prosecutions and some aspects of the poor law. The grants were designed to encourage better standards of provision in these fields and had grown steadily in amount. To place a limit on the cost of these grants to the national taxpayer, it was agreed that most of the specific grants mentioned above be replaced by a single combined grant, to be paid from a separate Local Taxation Account.

This Account was to be supplied with 40 per cent of the product of certain national taxes – the so-called assigned revenues. The system did not endure because the proceeds of the assigned revenues did not rise as fast as the expenditure of local authorities and because successive governments were unwilling to increase the range or percentage of the revenues paid to the Local Taxation Account. Although a failure, the assigned revenue idea is of much significance. It was an attempt to isolate central aid to local government from other types of national expenditure and thereby to reduce central supervision of local administration. It was also the start of a continuing argument about the relative desirability of general grants to local authorities as opposed to grants for specified purposes – a controversy examined more fully in Chapter 5.

As noted above, the reform of the small units of government in county areas was delayed until 1894. The urban and rural sanitary districts became urban and rural district councils of the pre-1974 model. In urban areas the change was little more than one of name. In rural areas the effect was more complex because the Local Government Act 1894 provided that a rural district area should not overlap a county boundary. Since the rural sanitary areas were based on the poor law unions which ignored county divisions, some reshaping of authorities was required. Rural districts acquired the duties of the rural sanitary districts, the highway responsibilities of the parish, or those of the highway districts where such existed. The relationship with the Poor Law Guardians was reversed. Previously the powers of the rural sanitary district were exercised by those Guardians representing rural parishes: after 1894 the rural district councillors also served as members of the Board of Guardians. The parishes were also overhauled and given, like the districts, a ratepayer franchise. However, the powers of the parish had largely been transferred to larger authorities. Some parishes were too small to justify the creation of a council: the Act decreed that parishes with 300 inhabitants must have a council, those with less than 100 could not, and those between 100 and 300 could choose. In the absence of a parish council, parish business has to be transacted at a parish meeting. London was left untouched in 1894. This final remnant of eighteenth-century chaos was removed by the London Government Act 1899 which replaced a miscellany of district boards and parish authorities in the LCC area by twenty-eight metropolitan borough councils, which were thought of as a counter-weight to the LCC which the Conservative government feared might become too powerful – a suspicion aggravated by what appeared to be its permanent Radical majority. Although the metropolitan boroughs were given responsibility for public health, housing, rating, libraries and recreational services, they never achieved parity of importance with the LCC. Due to the centralising tendency of modern times, as new duties were bestowed on local authorities they tended to go to the top tier, the LCC.

The passage of the London Government Act 1899 completed a new pattern of multi-purpose authorities elected on a ratepayer franchise. The complete system can be illustrated by a simple diagram.

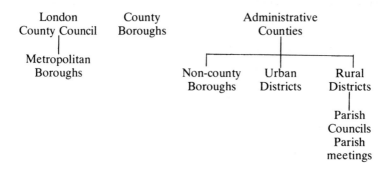

This structure remained until a fresh reform of London government took place in 1963.

Looking back over the nineteenth century it can be seen that it witnessed a constitutional revolution in local government. The public Bill steadily replaced the private Bill as the main instrument of change. A reconstructed system of elected, multi-purpose authorities emerged; the *ad hoc* principle went out of fashion. Separate organisations each devoted to a particular function have advantages. They can have areas most suitable for their particular purpose; they can generate specialised enthusiasm; they are not distracted by other tasks. However, the drawbacks of *ad hoc* bodies are substantial. They create a complex jumble of administrative units that is highly confusing for the public; if they are representative, the result must be a multiplicity of elections; the necessary co-ordination between them is difficult or impossible to arrange; either they cover a wide area and become remote or they are too small to use skilled manpower economically. Since the later Victorians were keener than we are now to uphold the representative principle, the move towards multi-purpose local authorities was wholly logical.

The intellectual forces advocating reform were powerful but not homogeneous. Sometimes they came in conflict with each other: this is one reason why the pace of change varied. The interaction of these ideas provides some explanation for the pattern of events and requires some attention.

The 1830s and 1840s were dominated by utilitarianism, the creed spread by Jeremy Bentham and his disciple James Mill. They argued that human affairs should be so organised as to secure the greatest happiness of the greatest number, that institutions should be judged by their utility, that is, by the extent to which they contributed to the sum of happiness. This is not the place to examine the philosophical and moral limitations of the utilitarian view: a study of local government must be concerned with its consequences. It was essentially a radical doctrine. It implied that existing arrangements and institutions should not be accepted unless they satisfied the test of utility. The chaos of local administration was so complete that patently it failed the test. But utilitarianism did not require a wide extension of the functions of the state. On the contrary Bentham tended to accept the principle of *laissez-faire* – that the government should leave things alone. State action was required only where it was necessary to increase the total of human happiness – if it produced more pleasure than pain. Today utilitarianism is out of fashion, partly because it is unsatisfactory in terms of ethics and partly because the measurement of pleasure and pain presents obvious difficulties. Nevertheless Bentham probably has a greater effect on contemporary thought and action than is commonly admitted. Of course, the concepts have evolved. Utility has been replaced by efficiency. Instead of a calculus of pleasure and pain, the modern calculus is of cost and benefit which can be measured, or estimated, at least in monetary terms.

Another influential concept was representative government. This idea has a long history. It had a great impact at the time of the English Civil War. In the eighteenth century the American colonists revolted over the principle 'no taxation without representation'. Any claim for representation raises immediate practical questions – who should be represented and how should their representation be organised? Throughout the nineteenth century an increasing number of public bodies were elected and the franchise was extended; in the early years voting was restricted to some ratepayers and the number of votes each enjoyed might vary from one to six depending on the rateable value of their property, but by the end of the period each ratepayer had one vote. So there was progress towards a ratepayer democracy. But those who urged the need for representative government were not necessarily favourable to democracy. It was widely accepted that those who contributed to the local rate should control the spending of the money raised. John Stuart Mill, the son of James Mill, argued convincingly that participation in the process of government was a valuable education in public affairs which helped to produce a sense of responsibility in the community and stimulated the creation of local leadership. Yet to give the vote to all implied that policy might be controlled by the wishes of uneducated people – and of people who contributed little or nothing to the rates but derived benefit therefrom. However, the franchise for both parliamentary and local elections was steadily widened, partly because any limit appeared arbitrary and ·was awkward to defend politically, partly through the rise in educational standards and partly because limitation of the franchise caused administrative difficulties.

Utilitarian philosophy and demands for representative government reinforced each other in national politics. At local level they tended to come into conflict, at least before 1861. Chadwick regarded local self-government as potentially a vehicle for corruption. Utilitarianism demanded some element of central supervision of local administration to ensure that it was adequate and competent. The claim that the ratepayers, or their elected representatives, should decide how much to spend and how to spend it could easily clash with attempts to impose national standards. Controversy of this nature was widespread in connection with the development of drainage and other environmental health services. And the wider the representation, the greater the proportion of the populace to have the vote, the more likely were such clashes to arise: the poorer classes were more willing to take their chance of cholera and other diseases if this meant paying less in local rates. Opposition to central control led to the break up of the Central Board of Health in 1858. However, John Stuart Mill's *Representative Government* published in 1861 modified utilitarian doctrine in that it accepted the need to work with and through educated local opinion.

The third powerful force in local government was a feeling of humanity. This is an ageless sentiment; throughout time there had been some compassion for the poor, the ailing and the disabled. In a period when the Christian religion achieved great strength, one would expect humanity to influence public policy. However, it easily comes into conflict with other principles and baser motives. The administration of the poor law provides a clear example. Utilitarianism required a rigid, controlled and harsh regime to reduce cost, to stimulate self-help, in order to produce the greatest happiness for the greatest number. A humanitarian approach needed more flexibility, more charity and more expenditure. The reform of the poor law in 1834 was a triumph for utilitarian principles but slowly these were softened by slightly more generous administration.

Humanitarian thought stressed the dignity of the individual. It

believed, to use a Victorian phrase, that people should be encouraged to better themselves. The argument can be presented with
varying emphasis and degrees of sophistication. It is better for the
country as a whole if everyone works hard to improve their position.
God has given to each individual certain potentialities – it is
therefore appropriate that these potentialities be used to the full.
The same view can also be put without reference to God. Thus a
climate of opinion was created favourable to state assistance to
education, an attitude powerfully supported by the obvious need for
a more highly skilled work force in an economy based on industrial
processes of growing complexity.

Agreement that the state should take steps to promote human
welfare necessarily required an erosion of support for *laissez-faire*.
This doctrine, widely accepted in the early years of the century,
argued that material prosperity was obtainable most speedily by
fostering the spirit of free competition and leaving every man to
work for his own interests. The role of the state, in this view, was
minimal, limited to the preservation of internal order and security
from external attack, and perhaps to provide bare essentials of life
for those manifestly too weak to enter into the mêlée to acquire
higher standards of comfort. But *laissez-faire* had no convincing
solution to the problem of poverty caused through unemployment,
to problems of public health or illiteracy. Even on questions of
economic organisation it could not apply to the provision of services
which required a heavy initial capital outlay and much interference
with public and private rights. Free competition between railway
companies, tramways, water and gas companies was obviously
wasteful and undesirable. If price competition forced down standards of maintenance of equipment, the result was public danger. So
the Victorians came to accept that there were natural monopolies
that had to be controlled by the state, or provided by public
authorities, to prevent exploitation of the consumer. Thus many
towns provided their own water and gas supplies and later in the
century electricity and tramways were added to the list of municipal
trading services.

Support for representative institutions and humanitarian and
utilitarian principles provided the driving force for change. But
powerful pressures also worked against reform and hindered
progress. Essentially these were the spirit of conservatism and the
inevitable unpopularity of raising more money through taxation.
These generalisations apply both to the nineteenth century and to
our own time. It is easy to argue that things should be left as they are;
that proposed changes are fraught with hidden difficulties; that the
benefit of reform is exaggerated in relation to its cost. These

attitudes will be promoted by wealthy persons and those in positions of authority who feel themselves threatened by change. Sometimes these established interests – Bentham called them sinister interests – have been so powerful as to be able to frustrate demands for reform: the history of the City of London in the nineteenth century is a paramount example of this situation.

PROPOSALS FOR CHANGE 1945–72

The patterns of economic and social affairs in Great Britain steadily become more uniform. The process can be traced back through the centuries but has been more pronounced in recent years. Technological progress has improved communications so distance matters less and less. It is much easier to administer large areas. The mass media aid public knowledge of what happens in other places. A better educated and more articulate public opinion tends to demand equality of treatment; if certain facilities are available in another county or another city, why are they not available here? This kind of pressure helps to involve the national political parties more deeply in local issues. Meanwhile the growth of local services has been so substantial that their total cost has a major impact on national resources. So the Cabinet of whatever party wants to try and steer local authorities towards policies that will not conflict with their own programme.

All these tendencies point towards a more centralised system of local government with fewer and larger local authorities. If uniformity is more highly regarded than local initiative, then less stress will be placed on the need to encourage local representation. Yet this line of thought conflicts totally with the philosophy on which the pre-1974 structure of local government was based. Its foundation was three Acts of Parliament passed at the end of the nineteenth century which were designed to ensure that local councils responded to the wishes of local ratepayers. Late Victorians insisted on ratepayer democracy. In geographical terms they commonly utilised boundaries which already existed, including county boundaries which can be traced back to feudal times. The structure as it stood in 1972 had been created in a different age for the needs of a different age, when the duties of local authorities were far more limited and before the internal combustion engine had revolutionised means of transport. Prior to 1972 little had been done to modernise the Victorian legacy. True there had been some changes. Between 1888 and 1929 just over twenty new county boroughs were created; in the 1930s the number of county districts was substantially reduced; boundaries of boroughs were widened to embrace advancing suburbia; some urban districts achieved the dignity of borough status and so became able to parade a mayor and aldermen on ceremonial occasions. But the pace of change has been slowed down by the clash of local interests, particularly between counties and boroughs. The counties managed to prevent the establishment of any new county boroughs between 1929 and 1964, motivated by the fear that new county boroughs would mean loss of some rateable value by the counties.

Thus the local government map failed to adjust to movements and growth of population. Anomalies inherited from the Victorians became more glaring while others emerged. In 1972 the largest administrative county, Lancashire, had a population over one hundred times greater than that of the smallest county, Radnor, and over eighty times greater than that of Rutland, the smallest English county. In the county borough class, Birmingham was thirty times the size of Canterbury. There were also second-tier authorities with a population three times that of Canterbury. Over thirty county districts, most of them in Wales, had less than 2,000 inhabitants. It was even possible to find third-tier authorities, suburbanised parishes in rural districts, with a population not far short of that of Radnor.

The existence of many small county districts had a profound effect on the allocation of local government duties. Legislation has assumed, with minor exceptions, such as libraries, that all local authorities of any one type must be given equal statutory rights in respect of any function. It was also held that functions cannot be subdivided, so that if a county must be given a particular part of a function, like education, it must have the whole of it. Yet highways were a notable exception to this rule. But the total effect was to drain functions away from the second-tier authorities and to change the pattern of local administration not by a comprehensive scheme of reform but by *ad hoc* measures relating to individual functions. Thus the second-tier authorities lost powers over elementary education, planning, fire service, personal health services and rural roads to the county councils. This aggravated tensions between counties and the larger county districts and led to demands for the delegation of county responsibilities to the larger districts – a clumsy compromise that often worked badly.

Another outdated concept that stayed until the 1972 Act was the differentiation between urban and rural districts. Nineteenth-century legislation was based on the belief that the countryside needed fewer services than the towns, notably in relation to sewerage. Subsequently the difference in powers between urban and rural districts was often reduced, but twin organisations with virtually identical tasks were often located in the same small town where an urban district or borough served an inner area and was divided by an antique boundary from the rural district serving the hinterland.

The main failing of the pre-1972 system, however, was that many of the top-tier units were too small. Specialised services which demand the use of highly qualified staff, purpose-built accommodation and expensive equipment can only be provided economically for a substantial population. Strategic planning cannot be effective unless it is designed to cover broad areas; the fact that county councils and county boroughs were separate and independent planning authorities inhibited the possibility of reviewing the development of adjacent urban and rural areas as a whole. The minimum size for top-tier units has been a matter of constant argument, but estimates continually increased. In 1888 the minimum population for county borough status was 50,000 and four exceptions below that figure were permitted. In 1926 the minimum was raised to 75,000; in 1958 to 100,000. In 1966 the Royal Commission on Local Government was told by government departments that top-tier local authorities should have a minimum population in the range 200,000 to 300,000; the County Councils Association, in their evidence to the Commission, envisaged half a million. Government departments are attracted by the idea of fewer and larger local authorities as being easier to supervise in the interests of uniformity. Local authorities slowly accepted the need for bigger units out of fear that they would lose functions to other sectors of public administration.

If the case for change was so strong – one may well ask why so much time elapsed before any effective reforms were achieved? What were the obstacles? Reformers commonly fail to appreciate the extent and value of local patriotism. Councillors who had given much devoted service to a local authority could not be expected to welcome its demise and tended to resent any implication that their council had not been efficient. Local government officers, especially chief officers, feared the effect of change on their personal status. Ratepayers often feared, without firm evidence, that proposed alterations would adversely affect the local rates. Behind these forces of local opinion stood the national pressure groups, the associations of local authorities, always ready to try to safeguard the interests of their members. Inevitably the different types of authority, notably counties and county boroughs, had opposing ideas as to the optimum pattern for local government; county boroughs favoured a single all-purpose authority while the counties urged the multi-tier system.

Successive Conservative and Labour Cabinets were weak in failing to insist on reform in the face of disagreement among the interested parties. As was seen in 1972, such disagreement is a help to a government that is determined to make changes. But before 1970 the reform of local government had a low political priority and ministers wanted to achieve a broad consensus before taking action. The topic was regarded as awkward. Many councillors are leading local personalities well able to make their views known to a local MP, and faced with sufficiently strong and influential local pressure a government backbench MP might even find it expedient to ignore the party whip in the House of Commons on this issue. And there is a great difference between accepting the need for reform in principle and accepting a particular scheme which would drastically upset the established arrangements for representation and administration in your own area.

The process of reform started ultimately in London. For a Conservative government the political strains here were much less. As the London County Council was commonly dominated by a Labour majority, a Conservative Cabinet had few political inhibitions about promoting change. In 1957 a Royal Commission had been established to study the special characteristics of the capital and the surrounding area which, therefore, was excluded from the operations of the English Commission established by the 1958 Act. The central difficulty in London was the absence of any local authority which embraced the whole of the built-up zone. The London County Council had inherited the 1855 boundary of the Metropolitan Board of Works which a century later had ceased to have any connection with geographical realities. No single local authority could have a synoptic view of the issues connected with the redevelopment of Greater London, the movement of population and the construction of main traffic arteries.

In brief outline this was the situation facing the Royal Commission on London Government. Its report, Cmnd 1164 of 1960, unanimously urged drastic changes. The Commission was of opinion that a Council for Greater London should be established to be responsible for overall planning, main roads, fire and ambulance services. It would also share responsibility for education, housing, planning applications and certain other services with a new type of second-tier authority – Greater London boroughs. These Greater London boroughs would have the status and constitution of municipal boroughs except that the City of London would be permitted to retain its ancient institutions. The Commission's scheme envisaged fifty-two of these boroughs with populations between 100,000 and 250,000 – except, again, for the City of

London: they would be responsible for health and welfare services, child care, local roads and libraries, in addition to the duties shared with the Council for Greater London. Reorganisation on this scale involved the disappearance of the LCC, Middlesex and three county boroughs, substantial loss of territory and rateable value by four county councils, and extensive amalgamations of county districts and metropolitan boroughs. These proposals aroused considerable opposition in the Labour Party and also in some suburban fringe areas which heartily disliked the prospect of integration with the metropolis.

In this instance, however, the government were not deflected by local hostility. They accepted the broad lines of the Royal Commission's report and the London Government Act 1963 now provides an opportunity for the co-ordinated planning of the whole metropolitan area. There were some modifications to the Commission's proposals. The number of London boroughs was reduced from fifty-two to thirty-two. There were two reasons for this change: first, some fringe areas were excluded from the London area altogether and remain in Surrey and Essex; and second, and far more important, the minimum population of London boroughs was doubled. This rise to 200,000 was due partly to the further decision that London boroughs shall have full powers over education – save in the former LCC territory where a committee of the GLC, the Inner London Education Authority, representing the area concerned, has this responsibility.

In provincial England there had been some half-hearted attempts at modernisation. A Commission established under the Local Government Act 1958 had managed to make some local adjustments, often in the teeth of strong opposition. Before long it was clear that the Commission was a broken reed, so in 1966 the Labour government nominated a Royal Commission to review the situation afresh.

The main issue facing the Commission was the choice between essentially one-tier and two-tier local government. Here a dispute arose between the Commission and one of their number, Mr Derek Senior. The Commission, except Mr Senior, proposed that the greater part of England be divided into fifty-eight unitary authorities which would be responsible for almost all executive action in relation to local government services. Unitary areas would embrace town and countryside. The major towns which provide a focus for the commerce and cultural life of the surrounding area should also constitute the centre for local government. The administrative map would be made to coincide as far as possible with contemporary economic and social geography.

Mr Senior's alternative was the concept of the City Region. He had advocated thirty to forty City Regions as the optimum basis for reorganisation before being appointed to the Commission. It is arguable that anyone already committed to a particular solution to a problem is unsuitable to inquire into it. Not surprisingly, Mr Senior pursued his idea of a City Region and became estranged from his colleagues. There is some similarity between his City Region concept and unitary authorities since both ensure the amalgamation of town and country. But the thirty-five Senior City Regions were larger: twenty of the thirty-five regions would have had virtually a million or more inhabitants. All members of the Commission were agreed that units of this size were too large to be all-purpose authorities and so the Senior plan proposed 148 second-tier district councils. The Senior City Regions would have been responsible for planning, transportation, water supply, sewerage, police, fire, education and 'capital investment programming': other more personal services would be left to the district authorities.

Public reactions to the unitary authority idea were hostile. The Conservative Party favoured a two-tier system. So also did the County Councils Association and the Urban and Rural Districts. Rural areas feel strongly that a two-tier system reduces the danger that the interests of the countryside will be disregarded and swamped by urban centres. Almost in isolation the Association of Municipal Corporations favoured the unitary scheme. There was much sympathy among local councillors for the Senior alternative because it provided for more local councils and seemed less remote, but this ignored the fact that the Senior scheme would have produced fewer and larger education authorities and that his proposed boundaries would do more to disturb present administrative and social patterns. All the pressure was for more representation, more 'democracy' and, in general, to water down the scale of reform. The election of a Conservative government in 1970 ensured that the concept of unitary authorities was dead.

The new government in 1970 grasped the nettle of local government reform with commendable vigour. The Ministry of Housing and Local Government was renamed the Department of the Environment to stress the breadth of its responsibility to promote good living conditions. Early in 1969 a Commission on the Constitution had been appointed with wide terms of reference – 'to consider the relations between the central government and the several countries, nations and regions of the United Kingdom'. Clearly, this broad inquiry would have provided a good excuse to postpone changes in the structure of local administration. The opportunity for delay was ignored. The new secretary of state, Mr Peter

Walker, moved ahead and quite rapidly prepared a fresh policy.

A White Paper published in February 1971, *Local Government in England* (Cmnd 4584), itself was remarkably brief. A mere dozen pages outlined the basis of a new system of local government. The detailed geographical application of these principles was set out in a separate document, Department of the Environment Circular 8/71. The White Paper recognised the ever-competing claims of efficiency, which demanded larger units of organisation, and representative democracy which favoured smaller units. A fair compromise had to be made between them but where the arguments were evenly balanced the White Paper promised that the case for fuller representation would be decisive. So the tasks of local government were to be divided between two tiers of authorities, counties and districts. The allocation of functions was to differ between the main industrial areas with heavy concentrations of population and the remainder of England which is predominantly rural or semi-rural. Thus there are two styles of local government system, the metropolitan and the non-metropolitan.

The crucial distinction between the two lies in the distribution of responsibility for education, including libraries, and the personal social services. It was argued in the White Paper that the effective organisation of these functions required a population between 250,000 and 1 million, although these limits were not to be rigidly applied. The minimum figure was substantially below that advocated by the Department of Education and Science in its evidence to the Royal Commission. In the conurbations it is possible to form second-tier districts compact in size which fall within this population range. Here the districts can undertake education and the social services. Six metropolitan areas were proposed – Merseyside, Greater Manchester, West Midlands, West Yorkshire, South Yorkshire and Tyneside.

In more rural areas the second-tier authorities must have a population far below 250,000 if they are to be reasonably small in area with offices readily accessible for residents and councillors. Here the major functions remain largely with the county council and the distribution of powers between county and district remains very similar to the previous pattern. A Boundary Commission was established to delimit areas for non-metropolitan districts and this body reported in 1972 with proposals for 278 districts with an average population around 100,000. As far as possible the new district map was formed by amalgamations of existing authorities. In the most remote rural areas district populations fall as low as 40,000. Largest districts are former county boroughs which the Commission felt unable to split, for example, Bristol, but the fledgling county borough of Teesside was divided into three districts. Subsequent negotiations secured some changes in the boundaries originally proposed, but in general, the original suggestions were carried into effect.

The White Paper recognised the value of the third-tier authorities, the rural parishes. These were to continue, but with powers rather than duties. But what was to be done with the boroughs and urban districts due to lose their separate identities in the reshaping of second-tier authorities? Subsequently it was agreed that third-tier councils be formed in many of the former boroughs and urban districts within an upper population limit of approximately 20,000. Areas which had formed larger authorities were held not to need separate institutions as they would play a major role within the new district councils.

For Wales the proposals of the Conservative government were in tune with their policy for England. The two-tier system was to prevail everywhere. The new pattern contained seven counties and thirty-six districts. Glamorgan was to be split into two and five other counties – Clwyd, Dyfed, Gwent, Gwynedd and Powys – were to be established broadly on the lines described above. The Local Government Act itself contained a further change: Glamorgan was divided into three sections. This further division is controversial because the new county of South Glamorgan is exceptional as it contains only two districts, one based on Cardiff and one on Barry. Cardiff dwarfs the remainder of the county. There are examples in England where a major city has a predominant position within a county but nowhere is this so overwhelming as in South Glamorgan. Whether Cardiff should have such exceptional treatment must be a matter of opinion.

The 1972 Act emerged after at least twenty-five years of intermittent official discussions about local government reform. Its passage to the statue book was relatively easy. The Labour Party opposed the Bill in Parliament, but the party's position was weakened by its earlier acceptance of the unitary authority plan advocated by the majority of the Royal Commission, an idea that was widely unpopular. Nor did Labour's other main objections to the Bill arouse much enthusiasm. To urge that metropolitan counties rather than districts should be given responsibility for education was to move against the current of opinion demanding fuller representation and participation. Another important criticism was that boundaries had been drawn too tightly around the metropolitan areas with the consequence that these authorities would find it difficult or impossible to obtain the land needed for housing development in the foreseeable future – at least within their own territory. Obviously the 'fringe' areas immediately affected did not share this attitude. They wished to remain as rural or semi-rural as possible and so were well content that the Bill excluded them from the conurbations. Indeed the final stages of the discussion were notable for a widespread feeling that change was inevitable and that the legislation must be allowed to pass.

Why was this fairly general acceptance obtained? In view of the tensions caused by earlier proposals this relative harmony demands explanation. One reason, certainly, was that a general weariness had surrounded the whole question. There was broad agreement that without reform local powers would be further eroded by central departments. Then the 1972 scheme was in many ways easier to accept than earlier plans. The Royal Commission had ignored the extent to which the county was a social unit as well as an administrative entity and that as a social unit it commanded considerable loyalty. In contrast the Conservative plan respected existing boundaries to a far greater extent, especially in relation to the counties. The associations of local authorities broadly accepted the plan with the exception of the Association of Municipal Corporations. And the AMC, although dissatisfied, was helpless.

So the Bill became an Act. The following chapters will outline the more important of its provisions.

Chapter 2

THE BASIS OF THE SYSTEM

TYPES OF LOCAL AUTHORITY

The reformed local government system in England and Wales is based on four sub-systems which can be illustrated conveniently by diagram. The structure for the main urban centres of population is shown on the left of the page and that for the remainder of the country on the right.

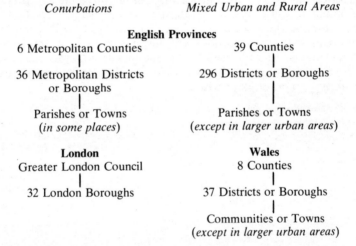

Conurbations	*Mixed Urban and Rural Areas*
English Provinces	
6 Metropolitan Counties	39 Counties
|	|
36 Metropolitan Districts or Boroughs	296 Districts or Boroughs
|	|
Parishes or Towns *(in some places)*	Parishes or Towns *(except in larger urban areas)*
London	**Wales**
Greater London Council	8 Counties
|	|
32 London Boroughs	37 Districts or Boroughs
	|
	Communities or Towns *(except in larger urban areas)*

In addition to these multi-purpose authorities there exists a wide variety of special purpose bodies and joint committees formed by or in association with the major local authorities. Perhaps the most important institution of this kind is the Inner London Education Authority (ILEA) which is responsible for education in all the inner London boroughs, that is, those which were within the area of the former London County Council.

Changes in the structure of local government have been evolutionary rather than revolutionary. The traditional units of local administration remain – the county, the borough, the district and the parish. A map showing the top-tier boundaries of today is recognisable as a development from a map of the traditional shires. Of course there are changes. The major centres of population have produced the new metropolitan counties and in rural areas the amalgamation of counties has produced Cumbria, the new enlarged county of Cambridge and the combination Hereford and Worcester. The face of Wales, in contrast, has been changed considerably with the large-scale amalgamation of counties and the trisection of Glamorgan. The greater part of England and Wales still has a three-tier structure. This apparently cumbrous arrangement provides for a fuller range of representation of local interests and opinion than would be possible with a simpler form of organisation. It also permits functions to be distributed between the types of local authority according to the requirements of a particular service: the allocation of functions is discussed in the following section of this chapter. Areas which have but two layers of local government are those in which an urban community itself forms a second-tier authority or which has such a strong position within a second-tier authority that it is not felt to need further, separate representation. The very smallest parishes, or in Wales the smallest communities, with a population below 300 do not have a council unless a parish meeting resolves to have one. Where the population is below 200 the consent of the district council is also required. Districts exercise some general supervision over their parishes, for example, in relation to boundary changes, elections and the compulsory acquisition of land. Where there is no parish council, the powers of the parish rest with an annual meeting which may appoint a committee to carry out any of its business.

Some districts enjoy the dignity of being boroughs. The chairmen and vice-chairmen of these councils are entitled to the status of Mayor and Deputy Mayor. To become a borough a district council must submit a petition to the Privy Council and the decision to do so must be supported by not less than two-thirds of the members voting thereon at a special meeting of the council convened for this particular purpose. If the view of the Privy Council is favourable, the district then receives a charter which may contain local provisions which appeared in earlier charters belonging to former boroughs now included within the district. In fact, every application received for borough status in 1973 and 1974 was accepted. And every metropolitan district except Sefton chose to be a borough. However, the practical effect of the powers of a district arising from borough status is negligible.

Great ingenuity has been devoted to the retention of the privileges of ancient boroughs. The 1972 Act provided three means to this end. Any parish or community council, that does not represent a grouping of parishes or communities, can resolve to choose the status of a town. This is a general right and is not restricted to former boroughs. When this course is adopted, the local council becomes a town council and the chairman of the council is entitled to be known as the town mayor. Thus former boroughs that still have their own institutions at third-tier level can retain something of their old status. It follows that an area can have two mayors, that is, wherever a parish which opts to be a town is included in a district which has applied to become a borough. But not all former borough and urban districts were permitted to have a separate third-tier council. The government ruled that such an authority should not have more than 20,000 population or alternatively not more than one-fifth of the population of the parent district council. These guidelines were applied with some flexibility: even so, at least 100 places were refused the right to have a parish or town council. Where a former borough is not allowed to retain a third-tier council, the method of preserving its dignities depends on whether the second-tier district authority becomes a borough. If it does, the charter rights and privileges transfer automatically to the new and larger borough. Where the district is not a borough, the district councillors elected to represent the former borough become charter trustees who are a corporate body, entitled to hold land and who can appoint one of their own number to be the town mayor.

One object which was prominent in the discussion which preceded the 1972 reform was the need to end the divorce between urban and rural areas. It was argued that a town which is a natural commercial, social and cultural centre for the surrounding hinterland should also be its administrative centre. At county level this aim has been achieved. At district level some authorities are wholly urban, some are essentially rural and some are mixed. The boundaries of many former county boroughs, now reduced to districts, were left unchanged in 1974. Extension of these towns to embrace adjacent rural areas would have created an obvious danger that the interests of rural communities would have been swamped by a dominant urban majority. So in some cases the distinction between town and country has remained at the second-tier level. Bath is a separate authority, an island wholly within another district: the same is true of Cambridge. Among third-tier authorities, the difference in status between town and parish tends to emphasise the urban/rural divide even more clearly than before the 1972 Act.

There are considerable variations in size within each category of local authority although these are far less bizarre than before the 1972 Act came into effect. Size can be measured in terms of acreage and population. Financial capacity is measured in terms of rateable value. Appendix A gives basic statistical information about the size of county and district authorities. Each metropolitan county exceeds 1 million population; the typical metropolitan district is nearer 250,000. Non-metropolitan counties average more than half a million people; a non-metropolitan district commonly has around 100,000 inhabitants. These figures give a general picture but there are extreme cases which depart a long way from the norms. The original intention was that the smallest non-metropolitan county should be Northumberland with a population of a quarter of a million. At a late stage in the passage of the Bill, the government accepted that the Isle of Wight should be treated as a special case owing to its physical separation from the mainland. So the island is now the smallest county with a population a little above 100,000. Bristol is a quite different type of unusual case. It is the largest non-metropolitan district with a population of 425,000 – more than twice that of many metropolitan districts which have much wider powers. In terms of acreage the largest authority is North Yorkshire. In England the average number of districts per non-metropolitan county is a little over seven. Essex, Kent and Lancashire each have fourteen districts, but Bedfordshire and Cleveland have four and the Isle of Wight only two. New Town areas are all within a single district with the one exception of the Central Lancashire new town based on Preston, Leyland and Chorley which is split between these districts.

The structure in Wales is similar to that in the non-metropolitan parts of England save that the minor local authorities are termed communities rather than parishes. Since the Anglican Church in Wales was disestablished in 1919, it is not fitting that a name associated with church organisation should be linked to a secular unit of local administration. The main difference is that Welsh authorities tend to be smaller in population. Powys, the former county of Radnorshire, serves only 18,000 people. The county of South Glamorgan is also unusual in that it has but two districts.

Local councillors are elected for a four-year term. Polling is normally on a Thursday. It is arguable whether apathy about local elections would be reduced by adopting the continental practice of voting on Sunday. The pattern of elections is not uniform. County authorities are elected as a whole in each fourth year after 1973 on the basis of single-member constituencies. In the districts the position is more complex. The rule in metropolitan districts is that a third of the councillors are elected in each year when there is not a county council election. Non-metropolitan districts are allowed a double choice. They can opt either for whole council elections, as the counties have, or they can have elections by thirds as in the metropolitan districts. Again, they can opt for single member wards or multi-member wards or some combination of the two systems. The original arrangements were made after consultations with local opinion, that is, with representatives of the former local authorities. So in these areas there may be an election each year or every other year. Under the former plan the election in three years out of four would be for district councillors; under the latter plan the timetable will run – county election, blank year, district election, blank year, county election, and so on. After 1974 any resolution by a non-metropolitan district to change the existing arrangements needs a two-thirds majority to succeed. Parish and community councils, like the counties, are elected as a whole for a four-year term. They may be divided into wards; this is unusual in rural areas but normal in small towns.

The choices facing the non-metropolitan districts are worthy of further discussion. The borough tradition of the three-member wards and annual elections is favoured by political party organisations as giving local enthusiasts a regular focus for political activity which is felt to be helpful in maintaining interest. Accordingly this arrangement had been adopted in areas where party intervention in local elections is strong. However the system has major disadvantages. It necessitates larger electoral divisions and makes it more difficult for councillors and election candidates to become known to local residents. It increases the difficulties facing a non-party candidate attempting to organise his campaign. An annual election is more costly and causes more disturbance to the regular flow of council business. And where a council is run on strictly party lines, if one party has a substantial majority it may be impossible to displace it at a single election, however badly it is beaten at the polls. An election at which the government is immune, even in the short term, is not an attractive concept. It must reduce public interest in the right to vote, as also does the greater frequency of elections. The one advantage that can be claimed for electing one-third of a council at a time is that it does provide some guarantee of continuity of membership and safeguards against the return of a very inexperienced assembly of councillors.

No advantage can be claimed for the London borough system of whole council elections based on multi-member wards. It increases the difficulty of communication between the individual councillor and his constituents. It magnifies the benefit gained by the majority party from our 'first past the post' electoral system. In such elections minority groups tend to be decimated. At the London borough elections of 1978 the winning party secured more than 85 per cent of the seats in no fewer than seven boroughs although getting, on average, some 57 per cent of the vote. Islington provided the extreme example: Labour got 96 per cent of the seats on the borough council with 49 per cent of the votes. Our elections are based on the theory that areas should choose representatives, not that an elected body should reflect the balance of opinion between parties. We remain tied to a concept inherited from an age when political parties in the modern sense were unknown. This is not the place to argue the case for proportional representation, but results like that from Islington are impossible to justify. A local authority subject to the overwhelming domination of one political group is unlikely to be a healthy body for it will be deprived of the benefit of vigorous public debate.

The representative responsibility of a county councillor may be more individual than that of a district councillor elected as one of three ward representatives for an urban area. The county councillor has to travel to the county capital to fulfil his duties and becomes something of an envoy to a higher authority: to a lesser extent the same is true of a parish representative on the district council. All this should mean that county elections are more keenly fought than other elections because the winners have functions which are more vital and important than those who serve on other types of local authority. In the past, county council elections have been more often unopposed than borough and urban district elections. The explanation is probably twofold: there is less party political activity in rural areas and because the county authority seems remote and distant there is less appreciation of the wide range of its activities. It still, however, remains true that the consultation of local opinion by county councillors can be a more complex activity than similar consultation in districts. Where a council is controlled by politics a councillor must pay attention to the views of his party colleagues and supporters. In rural areas, where politics are less pervasive, a county councillor will feel he should keep in touch with the attitudes of his parish councils, the district council and other local associations within his constituency. There is much overlapping of membership between the layers of local government in the counties. Some county councillors serve on district councils; many district councillors serve on parish councils.

In the historical chapter it was noted that parishes often resisted being drawn into larger authorities, partly because they resented the loss of independence but perhaps even more because it was feared that any co-operation with neighbouring parishes would prove disadvantageous financially. Today the administrative county acts as a financial pool for the county districts within its boundaries. Counties spend far more money than districts but the latter have the task of levying the local rate. The counties impose a uniform rate on the districts. In consequence the more wealthy areas of the county tend to subsidise less well-to-do places. A prosperous town will make a proportionately greater contribution to county revenue than the ratio of its population to that of the whole of the county. This situation can generate hard feelings. Every part of a county area will wish to ensure that it is enjoying its fair share of county expenditure. Equally, the claims of a county councillor to secure benefits for his area must be judged in relation to the needs of the authority as a whole. Very often the interests of the county, especially in planning matters, will diverge from more local interests. If county councillors feel a strong need to press 'constituency' questions, who is to protect the interests of the county? There are a number of possible safeguards. Where party politics are a dominant influence, the majority party, one hopes, will take a broad view. On items of expenditure the processes of financial control impose restraint. Elsewhere it may be that chief officials exercise considerable sway over the conduct of affairs and help to stifle unreasonable local claims.

Before 1972 a major difficulty facing local government was that administrative areas remained relatively static and failed to adjust to movements of population. The suburbs of an expanding town frequently spilled over its boundaries into the surrounding rural area. While this was both inconvenient and inefficient it also failed to arouse demands for appropriate adjustments to be made. Indeed, public opinion was likely to be aroused only when proposals were made to change boundaries. To work in the town and live in the adjacent rural district had a curious status value. Further, rateable values in rural areas were often lower for historical rather than practical reasons. An allied consequence of population movements in both urban and rural areas was that, as electoral divisions tended to be static, councillors came to represent very unequal numbers of electors. Ward councillors from decaying urban centres represented fewer and fewer people while those from the new suburbs were responsible to more and more. This produced undemocratic unfairness.

To deal with such matters in the future, the 1972 Act established two permanent Boundary Commissions, one for England and one for Wales. Each Commission must make regular reviews of district and county areas within every ten to fifteen years – or otherwise as the appropriate secretary of state may direct. Local authorities and the general public must be fully consulted during the progress of these reviews and any Orders authorising boundary changes will be submitted for parliamentary approval. Alterations in parish or community areas will be suggested by the parent district council for the approval of the Boundary Commission. Should a district fail to make proposals, then the Commissions have reserve powers to act in default. Similarly the Commissions are to review regularly the electoral areas within local authorities and must be consulted about proposals from non-metropolitan districts to alter the local method of election.

One anticipates that there will be a considerable amount of work for the Boundary Commissions. Because the 1972 reorganisation of districts was carried out at high speed, many existing boundaries, although unsatisfactory, were left unchanged both in the interests of immediate administrative simplicity but also, no doubt, in order to minimise objections to the whole scheme of reform.

COUNTY–DISTRICT RELATIONSHIPS

The harmony of a two-tier local government structure is greatly influenced by the quality of co-operation between county and district councils. Both represent local opinion, albeit over different areas. Both share functions, especially planning, which cannot be exercised independently of each other. They can achieve important economies if they agree to share specialised resources. Yet there are serious hindrances to co-operation, namely, separate institutional loyalties, sometimes party political differences and a widespread instinct amongst the district councils to preserve and insist upon their independence.

Closer relationships between the two tiers can be assisted through a variety of methods. There is some common membership between the two types of authorities as some councillors have been elected to both district and county councils. One local authority can provide goods and services for another; this provision facilitates joint purchasing arrangements, the joint use of computers and the employment of both district and county staff upon a particular project. Section 101 of the Local Government Act 1972 allowed one local authority to act as the agent of another local authority in the provision of services: the difficulties of this arrangement are considered below. Finally, two or more local authorities can appoint a joint committee to help them to find a common approach to particular problems.

After the reorganisation of 1974, counties formed liaison committees with their districts to discuss matters of mutual interest. These bodies were regarded as a necessary contribution to the creation of good public relations. They might cover a whole county or be limited to a single district. They might constitute a general forum of discussion on local government affairs or they can be restricted to a particular function. They are purely advisory and have no executive functions. It may therefore be difficult to find useful work for them to do. They can too readily be used simply to complain about what other people are doing or not doing. There are also problems of organisation. If a single committee is used to cover a whole county and the county has equal representation with each district, then the county will be heavily outnumbered. If county representation equals that of all the districts together, then the burden of attendance on county councillors will be severe. Again, if a county establishes a separate committee for each district then the cost is heavy in terms of the time of both county councillors and county officials. Necessarily this problem is aggravated in the counties with a large number of districts, for example, Essex, Hampshire and Kent.

The tendency has been for these liaison committees to disintegrate because there has been little they could do. Partly this is due to economic policies which have restricted the scope for bold, fresh initiatives by local authorities. There is also less interaction between authorities in relation to their well-established duties. Arrangements for district councils to maintain county roads on an agency basis are now less common. The Housing (Homeless Persons) Act 1977 has placed firmly on district shoulders the task of finding accommodation for those who need it: the relationship between district housing authorities and county social service departments has been thereby clarified. As is shown below, the overlap between district and county planning responsibilities has also been reduced.

Co-operation between counties and districts can still be important. The topics involved include the organisation of elections, including the preparation of voters lists, and the administration of superannuation funds. Such items are not controversial and any discussion about them can usually be conducted by officers. Indeed, the dialogue between the two tiers is tending to slip into the hands of the officials.

Some counties have decentralised the administration of a particular service, for example, highways. Such an arrangement may be accompanied by the establishment of area committees with responsibility for supervising the local operation of the county service. Where this is done the district councils may be invited to nominate a few members of the area committees, and so are given a modest opportunity to influence county policy. The joint committees described above should be carefully distinguished from area committees. The former are purely advisory bodies; the latter are sub-committees with some executive responsibility.

The problems caused by concurrent powers continue to give trouble. Such powers provide splendid opportunities for co-operation between counties and districts; equally they can provide a climate in which mutual inaction flourishes. The danger of inertia arises from the possibility that a council may lose enthusiasm for a service in the hope that the other tier will exert itself and carry the financial burden. The list of these concurrent functions includes museums, art galleries, the acquisition of land, clearance of derelict sites, health education, aerodromes, action in face of natural emergencies and provision for recreation. The catalogue does not include major local government services but in total it amounts to a significant opportunity to improve the quality of life. One method of avoiding friction over these shared responsibilities is for the two tiers to strike a bargain. Thus in Tyne and Wear the arrangement is that the county shall be responsible for museums and art galleries while the districts provide leisure facilities which cater for physical exertion unless a district asks the county to take over a major project which will serve needs from outside the district.

It was noted above that planning powers are shared between counties and districts: counties are responsible for the formulation of broad strategy and districts deal with individual development applications. Clearly there must be co-operation between the two tiers if this system is to work well. In particular, districts should not be allowed to ignore county policy when granting planning permission. To meet this situation the Local Government Act 1972 required that the more important development applications should be referred to the county. This arrangement caused delay and complaint about the duplication of bureaucracy: the employment of separate teams of planners which spend much time negotiating with each other is clearly wasteful. District councillors and planning staff are better informed about the local environment and local opinion than county personnel can be. So the Local Government, Planning and Land Act 1980 redefined the distribution of planning powers so that the districts are virtually unhindered in relation to planning applications, although they are expected to take heed of the county's overall strategy.

THE COMMITTEE SYSTEM

Even in the smallest local authorities – other than parishes – it is obvious that all the detailed consideration of business cannot be done at meetings of the full council. Accordingly, committees are established. The tendency is for them to grow in number and in authority. They consume a great amount of time of both elected members and officers. It is commonly said that the committee is the workshop of local government: certainly, a realistic appraisal of committee behaviour is essential to a full understanding of the practice of local administration.

In the interests of speed in decision-making, the 1972 Act increased the powers that can be given to committees and to officers. A local authority may delegate its powers to a committee, sub-committee, or an officer. Further, unless the authority otherwise directs, a committee may arrange for its powers to be discharged by a sub-committee or an officer: thus the principal *delegatus non potest delegare* is avoided. However, the full council cannot remit its power to levy a rate or raise a loan. In accordance with the Maud and Bains Reports (discussed in Chapter 7) the tendency now is for simplified structures with fewer committees and sub-committees and wider delegation. It is common practice to nominate a central committee, usually entitled Policy and Resources, to deal with major issues concerning the allocation of funds and to exercise a co-ordinating role of the work of the authority as a whole. The number of committees varies from council to council. Second-tier authorities in the shires tend to have fewer as they have fewer responsibilities. It is no longer usual to appoint a separate committee for each major function or local authority department. Instead the work of an authority is divided into broad 'programme areas' and a committee is allocated to each. The question then arises – can the ambit of a committee be too broad? This issue has arisen particularly with planning and transportation which some authorities have treated as one programme area to be controlled by a single committee; other authorities have felt the scope was too great for a single body and appointed separate committees.

The frequency of committee meetings also varies. They tend to be more often in the districts than in the shire counties. But every councillor knows that the routine timetable of meetings can be supplemented by others called for a special purpose. A committee once born becomes unwilling to die. It may be justifiable to have a separate body to consider a fresh and unexplored problem but when the new category of business contracts or becomes routine, the justification disappears.

Each local authority decides on the size of its committees. The larger the body, the wider the range of opinion and experience that can be represented on it. Conversely, the larger the body the smaller must be the scope for the average member to play a significant part in its work and the greater will be the cost in terms of time demanded of the elected members. Authorities in rural areas tend to have larger committees because there is pressure for the constituent geographical parts to be represented. Where a council is run on party lines the majority group will ensure that it has a political majority on each committee. Otherwise the selection of committee members should take into account their regularity of attendance and reputation with fellow council members. The central policy committee is the key committee of a council and the most senior and able members are usually selected to serve on it. .

Is it useful for local authorities to inject more outside blood into their proceedings? The law permits this to be done. A council may include on its committees, other than a finance committee, persons with full voting rights who are not members of the parent council, providing that such additional members do not form more than one-third of any committee. This practice of co-option from outside does enable local authorities to widen the range of specialised knowledge and experience available for their deliberations. Magistrates form one-third of every Police Authority but this is tantamount to the creation of a joint committee rather than co-option. Otherwise the practice is optional. It is commonly used on education committees and boards of school governors and managers. (There is a widespread misconception that co-opted members are mandatory for education committees.) But apart from education, this device is not much used. One reason is a feeling that it is undemocratic to give authority to persons who have not been popularly elected. Council members may think that they can get adequate specialised advice from their officers. They may also fear that co-opted members would outshine them in discussion and have an unduly dominant role in committee decisions. Critics have also said that the system can be abused – that where councils are run on political lines, co-option can be a method of compensation for defeated council candidates. One local incident is worth recalling. In 1972 the co-opted members of the Exeter education committee voted with the minority Labour and Liberal groups to elect another co-opted member, said to be a left-winger, as chairman of the committee. The Conservative majority on the city council, acting under the terms of the 1944 Education Act, thereupon successfully applied to the secretary of state for permission to dissolve and reconstitute their education committee. This was done to avoid a situation in which the education chairman would not have been a member of the city council and, indeed, would have been hostile to its political majority group. This was an exceptional occurrence. In general, the practice of bringing additional people into local committee work is valuable and should perhaps be used more widely.

Meetings of committees are held in an informal atmosphere. The chief officer responsible for the committee's business or a committee clerk will sit next to the chairman in a strategic position to offer *sotto voce* words of advice. If the body is small enough it will sit round a table. Smoking is permitted unless health warnings have had effect. At the first meeting in the council year the initial task is to elect a chairman. Where an authority is subject to political control the chairmen are chosen by the majority group – otherwise the choice depends on the interplay of personalities. The normal practice is to start proceedings by approving the minutes of the previous meeting. The other items on the agenda will be to consider developments in matters that have been previously before the committee, and new pieces of business. Information on these will either have been circulated beforehand in reports prepared by the officers or there will be a verbal report at the meeting. Sub-committee reports are usually introduced by the chairmen of sub-committees. The volume of papers circulated to members to prepare them for the business varies considerably; often it is very substantial. The Maud Committee on *Management of Local Government* reported in 1967 that one of the largest county boroughs sent out 700 sheets of paper a month to each member of the council and 1,000 sheets to those on the education committee. One wonders what proportion of the papers were read. Strenuous efforts have since been made to cut down the amount of detailed business submitted to committees, and to reduce the bulk of paper circulated. In the case of education, the status of the committee is protected by law: a local education authority is required by statute to refer all matters to its education committee and must consider the committee's recommendations before taking action, except in an emergency. So the content of committee work is mixed. It is desirable that they should concentrate on issues of major policy but much time can still be consumed on trivial items that become contentious, perhaps for political reasons.

Thus committees are separate but interrelated cogs in the local government machine. How can they be made to mesh smoothly together? This raises the allied problems of co-ordination and control. Such supervision is essential otherwise committees would become wholly independent entities. Control is vital to ensure that a council remains in full charge of its policies and expenditure. Co-ordination is needed to prevent waste. It need not involve saying 'No' to a committee, but is rather a matter of showing them that their proposals can be carried out more effectively or economically if they are done in a certain way. A problem facing one committee may already have been dealt with satisfactorily by another. One committee may find that a certain piece of land or property is surplus to requirements while another committee may be seeking to buy a similar property. At this level co-ordination is increasingly the task of chief officers although formal responsibility may rest with some form of central policy committee. At lower levels, for example, the need to maintain steady work flows for office and outdoor staff, the responsibility must rest wholly on officials.

Control of committee policy raises other issues. All spending is subject to review by auditors, internal and external, who provide a rigorous check against irregularity. The formal process of policy control takes place at council meetings at which reports or minutes of committees are presented for approval. Where a committee has delegated powers it will present a report of its actions for the information of council members and not for approval. Practice varies as to how detailed these reports are. For obvious reasons in the larger authorities the scale of delegation is greater and less detail can be included in reports if they are not to be unduly lengthy. At the full council meeting should members object to the way in which delegated powers have been exercised they can do nothing where the delegation is absolute. Of course, the council can always withdraw the delegation.

On matters that are not delegated the council can reject a committee's proposals or refer them back for further consideration. This occurs infrequently. Time at council meetings is not limited in any strict or formal sense, but the patience and energy of elected members are limited. Were a large number of recommendations to be challenged, then meetings would become unduly long. Even so, there will be many occasions when the specialised enthusiasms of a committee will be overruled on matters of principle, on issues that affect the business of other committees and especially on levels of expenditure. How is this done? Wherever a council is run on party lines, policy supervision can be expected to come from the dominant political group which will settle its internal disputes, if necessary, by vote at its 'caucus' meetings. In the absence of strong party loyalties, the situation becomes more flexible. The general policy committee can normally persuade a council to prune back any proposals for expenditure it considers excessive. The ultimate check to a commit-tee is imposed by the balance of opinion expressed in council debate. The council must always prevail in any fundamental clash with a committee because it holds the ultimate sanction of being able to replace recalcitrant committee members with others who will heed the views of the full council.

The committee system offers substantial advantages. It ensures that all business has been subjected to prior consideration before it comes to a council meeting and thus avoids hasty decisions. This process of pre-digestion should enable a council to devote its attention to matters of major important. Council members can specialise on particular aspects of the authority's work, thus helping them to make a valuable contribution to it. The specialisation also leads to a deeper sense of involvement and commitment; it heightens the sense of responsibility for the committee's work. And by narrowing the ambit of concentration for the elected member, the committee system enhances his education in administration. The informal atmosphere softens differentials in status and partisan opinions. So officers can intervene in discussion and offer advice to an extent that would be resented and thought improper at council meetings. And where a local authority is dominated by party loyalty, in the freedom of committee the members will not always talk and act in party groupings.

Since a council cannot take all decisions one obvious alternative is to transfer much decision-making power to an individual, be he official or elected member. But the wisdom of any one man (or woman) acting alone is open to doubt, quite apart from the force of the dictum that power corrupts. The committee enables power to be shared and brings together a variety of interests and experience which, in most cases, should produce a better and more acceptable decision. Not all members will play an equal part in moulding the collective mind of the meeting: there will be always a few who give a lead, either through stronger personality or greater experience and ability. An adviser to the committee, a chief officer, may often persuade it. In these circumstances a committee decision is perhaps not a genuine collective decision, but is rather a 'front' or support for those people who dominate its deliberations. Yet a committee, unless completely inert, is a valuable check. The leading voices still have to convince. Without committees, far more decisions would be made without potential challenge.

Equally committees are open to criticism. There must be a tendency for each one to live in a world of its own, deeply conscious of its special problems but failing to see them in the context of the full responsibilities of the council. They may be swayed too easily by the advice of officials, backed by the authority of professional qualifications which can produce undue enthusiasm and ill-balanced judgement. There is always a danger that a committee may seek to build an empire and be over-concerned with matters of status. The safeguards are to establish a central policy or executive committee to oversee other committees and to have as few committees and departments as possible. Thus the Seebohm Report of 1968 recommended that all social services provided by local government be administered through a single committee: this idea became a requirement in the Local Authority Social Services Act 1970.

It was noted above that the power to delegate decisions to the committees is widely used. But how far should committees themselves deal with the detailed application of general policy, or how far should these matters be left to officials? The extent to which officials are permitted to act will vary. In larger authorities, delegation to officials has increased both in order to save time and to prevent committees being overburdened with detail. But there is some unwillingness among elected representatives to surrender prerogatives. There is a widespread conception of local democracy, dating from the Victorian era, which insists that it is the duty of elected representatives to take all decisions; that it is undemocratic to allow officials to exercise discretion. And some councillors do not wish to surrender matters to officials because they like dealing with details and personal cases.

A substantial cost has to be paid for any insistence that elected representatives must take decisions. Committee meetings are longer; sub-committees multiply; mounds of paper are distributed to explain the detailed business to committee members; officials spend much time in preparing these papers; if they are conscientious, committee members must spend time on studying agendas and reports; decisions are delayed until committees, and sometimes the full council, have met. All this might be tolerable were it certain that decisions would be made under optimum conditions. Unhappily this is not the case. Often elected representatives may be less qualified to take decisions than the officers who advise them. This statement has an undemocratic flavour but frequently it must be true. Normally a happy marriage between democratic principle and expertise is possible since committees accept the advice of their professional staff. A committee would not dispute the view of its surveyor that a bridge was unsafe. School governors and managers commonly think it improper to intervene on questions of curriculum. Yet this self-denying convention may break down. What is the best course of action to take in relation to a child in care? Here any committee member may feel that his opinion is as valuable as that of an official. When a committee is faced with an aesthetic issue it is a matter of opinion whether professional advice should necessarily be followed. There is great variety in the extent to which elected members concern themselves with staff appointments, including teachers: it is arguable that this is a type of responsibility that chief officials should be expected to shoulder. There is a danger that when committee members become involved in personal cases emotion may determine action, or an undesirable element of patronage or even corruption may creep into council business. Housing is an obvious example. If council tenancies are decided by officials operating a points scheme, no favouritism is likely to arise; if a housing committee or sub-committee arranges tenancies, the basis of decisions becomes a matter for speculation.

Over-devotion to detail gives elected representatives inadequate time to concentrate on major matters of policy. Committee members snowed under with papers containing information on trivial matters will have less time to read more important documents, for example, ministry circulars. Indeed, where circulars are not immediately relevant to committee business, members may never know of the existence of a circular or will not appreciate its contents. Likewise at meetings, if hours are consumed by the minor items on the agenda, inadequate time is left for important business. A wily official may put a difficult matter of policy at the end of an agenda in the hope that he can persuade a tired committee to follow a certain line of action. Some committees, the weak committees, may prefer to take time over fairly routine items and then get through the major business rapidly by following the advice of their staff because the major items are too complex for members to be able to debate effectively.

In theory, one can argue that committees should decide policy and leave their officials to carry out the details of administration. In practice, the distinction between policy and administration can never be clear-cut. At what stage does a decision on how to put a policy into practice become itself a policy decision? If unexpected administrative difficulties develop which involve additional expenditure, the elected representatives must be consulted. If the operation of a policy incurs unexpected difficulties with the public, the councillors will need to know.

Under the reformed local government system the local authorities are fewer in number and larger in size, so councillors must place increasing trust on the judgement of their officers. This principle is now widely admitted, even where the need for it is regretted. But not all the problems raised in this chapter can be solved by leaving matters to officials. The influence of the Bains Report on the relationships between committees and chief officers is discussed in Chapter 7.

STANDING ORDERS

Methods of procedure in local government are necessarily more complex, some would say clumsy, than the administrative processes in industry or commerce. Since local authorities spend public money they have a special duty to see that it is properly spent: risks which are commonly taken by private enterprise are less acceptable in public administration. The other difference is that local councils reach decisions after discussion, much of which is held in public, because in a democracy the public have a right to know how public business is being conducted. So to ensure that their affairs are conducted in a regular and orderly manner, local authorities draw up Standing Orders to regulate their own conduct. These are in addition to the statutory controls in the law of local government and they must not, of course, transgress statutory provisions.

Standing Orders are mainly concerned with laying down rules of debate and with the procedure for using the council seal and for dealing with tenders and contracts. The form of Standing Orders varies very much between authorities so that no detailed description would have general application. However, they will always govern the order of business at council meetings and how various types of motion of amendments may be moved. Some councils impose a time limit on speeches. This raises a number of issues: how much time should each member be given; how much preferential treatment, if any, should be given to the chairman of a committee or the mover of a motion; how far should there be a right of reply? It is much better to avoid any time limits, but this may not be possible in large authorities or where debates are animated by political differences. The major item of business at a normal council meeting is the consideration of minutes or reports from committees. Again, this can be organised in various ways. Committee chairmen may present their minutes or reports in turn and any questions or arguments about committee proposals may be allowed when the council is asked to approve them paragraph by paragraph. The danger of this method is that the council may spend an excessive amount of time on the affairs of those committees which happen to come early on the agenda. To try to obviate this imbalance of attention, Standing Orders may lay down an alternative procedure. This often takes the form of requiring the Clerk to read through the numbers of the paragraphs of each committee report: a member may interrupt to ask a committee chairman a question on the contents of a paragraph, but if he wishes to start an argument and challenge policy, he will say simply 'Object'. Then when the Clerk has finished reading through the paragraph numbers, the council proceeds to discuss the items to which objection has been taken. In this way members can get a conspectus of the total amount of contentious business before them and this may help them to use debating time more sparingly and effectively. Standing Orders can also guard against another danger – that a council will be rushed into hasty decisions without adequate prior consideration. There is a statutory rule that a county or district council cannot consider any business unless it has been specified in a notice summoning the meeting sent out three days in advance.

This rule may be modified by local Standing Orders which may also extend the principle to committees. They also contain provisions to support the authority of the Chair in moments of disorder, may provide for reception of petitions and deputations, and govern relationships between a council and its committees.

A main concern of Standing Orders is to maintain probity in local administration. They may incorporate rules about the declaration of interests by both councillors and officials. They will prescribe how tenders shall be invited and the form of submission. A general instruction is that the amount of a tender shall be treated as confidential in order to secure genuine competitions among contractors. Conditions may be laid down to require compliance with specifications issued by the British Standards Institution. There is some feeling that Standing Orders may be unduly restrictive and inhibit the development of efficient purchasing procedures. They also define the extent and the circumstances under which the authority's powers may be delegated.

Standing Orders are a vital element in the constitution of a local authority. They help to ensure harmonious operation and financial regularity. It is, of course, essential that they are understood both by elected members and by officers in positions of responsibility. Officers must observe the detailed regulations covering contracts and financial management; elected members will not be able to play a full part in discussion unless they know when and how they may intervene.

THE ASSOCIATIONS OF LOCAL AUTHORITIES

Towards the end of the nineteenth century each category of local authorities formed an association for mutual support and assistance. The 1972 reorganisation also provided a unique opportunity to reform these associations. One possibility was that they might join into a single body, perhaps with a federal constitution. The advantages of such a move were apparent. There would be a great simplification in the structure of the joint organisations which the associations had formed or on which they were represented. The development of further nationally based services to local councils would be facilitated. There would be administrative economies. Above all, local government would be able to speak to central government and the general public with a single and far more powerful voice. Discussions were held between the associations to see if a basis of unity could be found. However, no agreement was reached largely for political reasons. All the metropolitan counties and most of the metropolitan districts returned Labour majorities at the 1973 elections. So the leaders of these councils came to favour a separate national organisation for metropolitan areas in the knowledge that such a body would normally be dominated by the Labour Party. The Greater London Council, which previously had stood apart from the associations, agreed to join. So also did the London boroughs. Thus the Association of Metropolitan Authorities was born. When it became clear that unity among all types of authorities was impossible, the shire counties formed the Association of County Councils and likewise the districts formed the Association of District Councils. The third-tier authorities are now represented through the National Association of Local Councils which serves parish councils, town councils and community councils in Wales.

These associations have a wide variety of functions. They provide advice for individual local authorities. They give an opportunity to exchange opinions and experience about current problems. They provide representation on the wide range of public bodies and advisory committees that are in some way connected with local government. They co-operate with each other and so provide a united policy for some aspects of local administration. The associations nominate representatives on the myriad of National Joint Councils which bargain over salaries, wages and conditions of employment for all those on the payroll of local authorities.

The main task of the associations is to negotiate with each other and with government departments about proposals to change the law or any administrative practices concerning local government. In particular they engage in detailed negotiations with civil servants over the amount of financial assistance local government is to receive from the Exchequer through the rate support grant. Each association is in touch with a number of MPs and peers who may be asked, on appropriate occasions, to put forward in Parliament the point of view of a particular category of local authority. It is easy to overlook these activities and to underrate their significance, because much of the work is done in private and does not receive great publicity. In fact, central departments do not generally introduce a change in policy – unless it be a major political decision – without some prior and semi-confidential discussions with the associations. Should the latter be firmly united in opposition to government proposals, then ministers often make adjustments so that their policy becomes more acceptable. While the associations are often in conflict with government departments, every effort is made to keep relationships as harmonious as possible. They try to evade issues which are not strictly local government matters and they also avoid becoming entangled in a dispute between any one local authority and a ministry unless there are general principles involved of general concern.

Nevertheless, the growing tension between local and central government has soured relations between the associations and Whitehall. There is a growing belief that senior civil servants press ministers to get more powers to supervise local administration. And attempts by ministers to restrain public expenditure necessarily produce confrontation with the associations. Where an association is controlled by supporters of the central government, a conflict of interest within the majority group will emerge. Should the policy be to preserve party unity and accept ministerial views or should the policy be to stand up for the independence and aspirations of local government?

The growth of party loyalty in local government has had a significant effect on the way the local authority associations operate. The tendency is for each political group to meet separately before each formal committee and executive council meeting. The advice offered by the officials of the associations is tempered by knowledge of the probable attitudes of the political majority. Senior officials of the associations have less personal influence than in earlier days when the party element was much weaker. Conversely, the elected leaders of the associations have become more important. It was widely reported in 1980 that an agreement between Mr Heseltine, Secretary of State for the Environment, and Sir Gervais Walker, then Chairman of the ACC, was instrumental in avoiding defeat of the Local Government Bill in the House of Lords, as ACC pressure on Conservative peers to oppose the Bill was subsequently withdrawn.

Partly loyalty is still not as pervasive in the associations as it is in many local authorities. Councillors who attend association meetings have a primary allegiance to their own authority. The party groups in the associations have whips, but the whips are in no position to enforce discipline; the whips can try and persuade but they can never insist. The meetings are not gatherings of the party faithful but rather of ambassadors from separate institutions. In consequence the opinions of the associations on issues of secondary importance are not always predictable. Chairmen of association committees are less willing to exercise discretion than chairmen of local authority committees because they are less able to predict the attitude of members.

The associations have formed a number of joint bodies each with a specialised purposed and known by a code name devised from the initial letters in the formal title of the organisation. A glossary may be useful:

CCLEA   Central Council of Local Education Authorities
CCLGF   Central Council on Local Government Finance
JACLAP   Joint Advisory Committee for Local Authorities Pur-
         chasing
LACSAB   Local Authorities Conditions of Service Advisory
         Board
LAMIT   Local Authorities Mutual Investment Trust
LAMSAC   Local Authorities Management Services Advisory
         Committee
LGTB   Local Government Training Board.

The first two of these bodies require particular attention. The first enables all education authorities to meet together, discuss common problems, evolve common policies and press agreed positions on ministers and other bodies connected with educational development. No other local authority service has a separate organisation of this importance. CCLEA was established in 1974 when it effectively took over the functions of the Association of Education Committees; the AEC was formed in 1902 at the time of the Balfour Education Act and over the years had been a highly influential body. CCLEA is a joint undertaking of the ACC and AMA. These bodies are often controlled by opposed political parties. To avoid party wrangles there is a tendency for CCLEA to keep away from educational issues that involve a clash of political principle, for example, assisted places in private schools. CCLGF, created in 1975, differs from all the other bodies noted here because of the extent of participation by the central government. The chairman is the Secretary of State for the Environment. He is supported by other ministers and officials from this department and all the other government departments concerned with local government. Initially this body was regarded as an opportunity for consultation. In practice it has tended to become a forum where ministers make pronouncements on policy. It also forms working groups of central and local officials which undertake complex negotiations about level of local expenditure and the size and distribution of the rate support grant. It is arguable that local representatives do not handle these negotiations very well. Instead of working together to challenge the method of ministerial proposals, each interest group attempts separately to increase its share of whatever finance the government chooses to offer. The tendency is to scramble for scraps. Greed is more potent than principle. In such an atmosphere it is not too difficult for Whitehall to divide and rule. There is some element of secrecy surrounding this business. Ministers and civil servants hope that an air of confidentiality will reduce the party political element in discussions: local authority representatives hope that a cloak of confidence may make their representations more effective because central government are more likely to concede points in private than in public. Without doubt the CCLGF, together with its various subgroups, provides the major forum for the interchange of views between central and local authorities. It symbolises the tendency to centralise local affairs.

Chapter 3

FUNCTIONS

THE ACQUISITION OF POWERS

Local authorities derive all their powers from Parliament. This principle is central to the British system of government for we live in a unitary state in which the will of Parliament is supreme. The central legislature distributes powers and, equally, it can take them away. There are three types of local power, that which requires action, that which permits action at local discretion by a specified category of authorities and that which authorises a particular council or group of councils to do certain things. The first two stem from Public Bills introduced into Parliament by the government; the third requires a Private Bill sponsored by a local authority.

Local government law is complex, partly because it is detailed and partly because certain aspects are frequently amended. There is also a variety of legal forms. There is the basic law, now the Local Government Act 1972. London is treated separately so the Greater London Council and the London boroughs received their powers from the London Government Act 1963. The Local Government, Planning and Land Act 1980 is an example of an amending statute which affected many aspects of local government without changing the basic structure. More generally, however, powers are obtained from general Acts relating to a specific local authority function; obvious examples are the major statutes relating to public health, education and town and country planning.

Most of the duties conferred on local authorities by Parliament are mandatory, that is, compulsory, but in a few matters of secondary importance there is a choice of whether to use or 'adopt' powers. The Small Dwellings Acquisition Act 1899, which enabled councils to provide mortgage loans to encourage home ownership, is an example of this optional arrangement. Another more recent case is the ability of the rating authorities to decide under the terms of the Local Government Act 1966 whether to levy rates on unoccupied properties. In 1963 Parliament gave local authorities a general optional power to spend a penny rate in any way for the benefit of its area provided that such activity was not subject to other statutory limitations: the 1972 Act increased the permitted rate to two new pence.

A third type of power is that conferred by a local Act, where Parliament has accepted a request by a local authority to give it additional authority. The procedure for obtaining such special powers is complicated and expensive; generally speaking, only the larger authorities seek to promote their own Private Bills. A few pioneering ventures, notably the Birmingham Municipal Bank, have been started in this way, but much of the content of Private Bills is minor or technical and raises no issue of principle. The powers are of two kinds. They may give extra powers to a local authority to do things itself or they may permit the local authority to control the activities of others. Examples of the former relate to the Birmingham Savings Bank and the Brighton Marina. Examples of the latter include the control of local authority property and facilities. Just occasionally provisions in a Private Act are felt to have worked so well that they are transferred to general legislation: the Plymouth powers for controlling taxis were so used.

There is a strong case for a drastic simplification of local legislation. The Local Government Act 1972, section 262, required local authorities to review the need for special local powers. Each county works together with its districts to produce a fresh version of local Act powers that are still needed. The metropolitan counties have completed the process and have promoted new Bills which repealed provisions no longer required. The shire counties are intended to do the same by 1984. In 1981 the government produced a general enabling measure which conferred on local authorities those private Bill powers which experience had shown to be useful.

Private Bill procedure, if widely used, could have greatly broadened the span of local government. Perhaps this is why Parliament has ensured that the promotion of a private Bill is a formidable obstacle race. A resolution to promote a Bill must be passed at two council meetings by a majority of the members and public notices must be issued indicating the nature of the powers a council hopes to acquire. If all these hurdles are surmounted, a private Bill goes before Parliament where, having been scrutinised by a body of Examiners to see it is in appropriate form, it then has to go through the usual routine of three readings in both Houses. Normally these readings are a formality. Discussion is usually restricted to the committee stage which is held before a small group of Members who sit in a quasi-judicial capacity hearing arguments in support of the Bill and any objections to it. Pleadings for and against a Bill are undertaken by members of the 'parliamentary bar', a special kind of barrister. The need to employ these parliamentary counsel adds greatly to the cost of the proceedings, especially if a Bill arouses objections and the committee stage is protracted. It was shown above that a Bill will not succeed if it incurs ministerial hostility; however, ministerial support is not an absolute guarantee of success, especially as the Bill has to satisfy the Lords as well as the Commons. The Conservative interest in Parliament has tended to be hostile to new extensions of local authority activity, notably in relation to municipal trading.

GROWTH OF SERVICES

Throughout the twentieth century there has been a sustained growth in local authority services. Naturally, the rate of progress fluctuated. It was held back during both World Wars and advanced strongly afterwards. How far the need for local services is accepted and acted upon must be governed by the state of political opinion. The dominant tendency has been to agree to an ever wider range of social provision, to try and ease social and individual problems through facilities paid for out of the public purse.

Local services fall into four broad categories which may be termed protective, communal, personal and commercial. The following paragraphs illustrate these distinctions.

The first group of services is designed to protect the individual from a variety of dangers, for example, fire, assault, robbery and epidemics. Thus local authorities provide a fire brigade, a police force, refuse removal, food inspectors and weights and measures inspectors. These protective services constitute some of the older branches of local administration, although rural areas lacked a comprehensive fire service until 1938 as before then much reliance was put on voluntary arrangements. Protective functions are negative in character as they promote good via the suppression of evil. All are highly necessary but scarcely exciting. The licensing of theatres, cinemas and of other premises for music and dancing has dual purpose. It is a safety measure and is also used to protect public morals. A local authority can prohibit the public exhibition of a film it judges to be offensive: this creates anomalies since licensing authorities do not always take the same view about the same film.

Communal services again provide benefit for all, but in a more positive way. In earlier centuries trade and travel were assisted by parish responsibility for the roads. The towns repaired and lighted the streets. Today the geographical distribution of population and employment is guided by planning authorities, the beauty of the countryside is protected and facilities are provided to assist in its enjoyment. Parks and sports grounds are also provided, particularly in urban areas.

Personal services are of direct assistance to those individuals who need them. They form the most costly sector of local government functions. Education is the most expensive item. Other personal services include welfare services for children, the aged and the disabled. The use of these is optional. A parent need not send his children to a local authority school. A frail old lady living on her own need not apply for a home help. But the percentage of people who decide not to make use of public services is declining. Some services are free; others are partially subsidised. All are financed from the local rate fund supplemented by national grants. Where a charge is made, for example, home helps, it may be wholly or partly remitted subject to a means test. Thus the personal services have an important equalising effect on society in that they benefit the poor at the expense of the rich – or the richer; they benefit the sick and the family man at the expense of the healthy and the childless; they benefit those who use public services at the expense of those who do not, although entitled to do so. Over the years the development of free services has been urged forward by left-wing opinion. There is now pressure for these benefits to be provided on a selective basis so they are paid for by people who can afford it. Local authorities are tending to operate the means test principle more fully.

Trading services have declined since the nationalisation of gas and electricity in the postwar period. In 1974 water undertakings were transferred to the new Regional Water Authorities. However, in London and the metropolitan counties local authority control over passenger transport has been strengthened in recent years. Many local councils also subsidise passenger services, but this is a social welfare provision not a trading activity!

The division of local functions into these four groups is useful for the purposes of analysis, but the allocation of a particular service between the groups can be a matter of opinion. In a sense, all of them are communal. Education is provided for individuals, but it is a matter of communal benefit to have an educated society. And whether housing is regarded as a personal service or a trading undertaking must depend on how far council tenants pay an economic, that is, unsubsidised, rent. Clearly, the sale of council houses is a trading activity. A few years ago it was arguable that town and county planning should be termed a protective service since it concentrated on stopping bad things, for example, ribbon development; now it promotes environmental improvement and should be classed as a positive communal service. The introduction of tolls on new bridges is something of a reversion to the turnpikes and produces the flavour of a trading service.

In terms of expenditure, there is great inequality between local services. As noted above, education is easily the most expensive;

broadly speaking, it costs about as much as all the other local activities. The service has improved steadily in extent and in quality. At the end of the nineteenth century the school-leaving age was 12; it was raised to 14 in 1900, to 15 in 1939 and 16 in 1973. The old School Boards had been given powers to provide 'elementary' education and this was commonly defined as being limited to basic skills of reading, writing and arithmetic. Indeed, in a famous judgement in 1901, the Cockerton case, a court ruled that the London School Board had no right to provide advanced courses. As the leaving age had been recently raised to 14, this judgement provoked an immediate crisis that demanded instant action. The Education Act 1902 abolished the School Boards and their powers passed to the multi-purpose authorities. The counties and county boroughs received powers to provide more advanced or 'secondary' education and some pupils began to stay at school until the age of 18. In the nineteenth century the public libraries developed in urban areas but an Act in 1919 extended the service to the whole country. The Education Act 1944 required local education authorities to provide secondary education for all pupils. All the time there has been a development of post-school courses in technical colleges, schools of art, teacher training colleges and, more recently, colleges of higher education and polytechnics. The education offered has been of ever more advanced standards. This tertiary sector of education now provides courses leading to degree qualifications.

In the Victorian period the care of the poor was regarded as a major task for local administration. However, the abolition of the Poor Law Guardians was recommended in the 1909 Report of the Royal Commission on the Poor Law; the idea was that their duties should be passed over to the multi-purpose authorities, just as those of School Boards had been seven years before. No action was taken on these lines because the Liberal government was unwilling to entrust the care of the poor to county councils, most of which were deeply Conservative in outlook. So the Guardians survived for twenty years more. In the 1920s more Unions were controlled by Labour majorities; these were accused by their opponents of extravagant expenditure. The Popular Guardians led by George Lansbury at one stage refused to pay their share of the expenditure of the London County Council owing to the high cost of poor relief in Poplar. Allegations of corruption by the Guardians were widespread. An Act passed in 1926 gave the Minister of Health power to take over the duties of the Guardians if he found their administration to be defective: this was done in three places, Bedwellty, Chester-le-Street and West Ham. Ultimately the Guardians disappeared in 1930 under the terms of the Local Government Act passed the previous year. Their duties were taken over by the county councils and county boroughs and divided up between committees dealing with health, education and public assistance. The latter function was transferred to central government agencies in two stages with the establishment of the Unemployment Assistance Board in 1934 and the National Assistance Board in 1948. Also in 1948 came the final break up of the poor law when the Children Act and the National Assistance Act redefined the powers of counties and county boroughs to care for children, the aged and the infirm.

Personal health services remained in an administrative tangle until 1946. Hospitals had three origins – voluntary organisations, the Boards of Guardians and public health authorities. The Guardians were concerned with medical services for the poor while the health authorities were required to isolate persons suffering from infectious disease. After 1930 the medical wards of workhouses were taken over by the health committees of the counties and county boroughs and turned into general purpose hospitals. County boroughs, counties and some other boroughs and urban districts were made responsible for maternity and child welfare from 1907 onwards and had opened clinics for this purpose. The National Health Service Act 1946 transferred all hospitals to the new Regional Hospital Boards, but an expanded range of medical and social duties, including the aftercare of hospital patients, the provision of health visitors and home helps was allocated to counties and county boroughs.

The construction of council houses and flats was started before the end of the nineteenth century. It was then thought of as an aspect of public health because the slums were breeding-places for disease and their progressive replacement was a medical requirement. After the First World War the public provision of housing was accepted as a social need, and various Acts were passed which gave national financial assistance towards council building. Housing powers went to the boroughs, urban and rural district councils. This is the one modern service not allocated to county councils. Indeed, without the housing function it is difficult to see how many district councils could now justify their existence. Until 1977 housing authorities had powers rather than obligations. They could provide council houses; indeed, they were expected to provide houses. But no one could claim a right to council accommodation. The Housing (Homeless Persons) Act 1977 changed this situation. Now a housing authority has a duty to provide accommodation for homeless persons. The duty is subject to a variety of restrictions; it applies only to those normally resident in the area and anyone who has deliberately made himself homeless loses the right to assistance.

This Act, combined with the reduction in council house building and the sale of council properties, has reduced the chance that those on the ordinary waiting list for council houses will get a home.

In the 1920s there was a great rise in the popularity of motoring. The increase in traffic created demands for higher standards of road maintenance. It will be remembered that highways were then the responsibility of the boroughs and districts, save that the counties maintained the more important 'county' roads. The Local Government Act 1929 sought to improve the state of the roads in the countryside by transferring the powers of rural districts to the county councils. Towns with a population above 20,000 were allowed to 'claim' highway powers over county roads within their boundaries and all urban authorities remained responsible for minor roads. Trunk roads were first designated as such after 1936 and in the 1960s modern motorways began to appear. Heavy freight traffic was moving from the railways to the roads. The government accepted financial responsibility for these major routes of national importance but county authorities were still used as agents for much construction and maintenance work.

Town and country planning is a further example of the transfer of functions to the higher tier of local authorities. All the earliest planning legislation from 1909 to 1932 had given boroughs and districts the opportunity to introduce local planning schemes. But this multiplicity of planning authorities proved a serious hindrance to the effective control of development – there were, for example, 133 planning authorities in the area served by London Transport. In fact, only a small part of the country had been covered by operative planning schemes prepared by borough and district councils, partly because of the intricate procedure and also due to fear of liability to pay compensation. The Town and Country Planning Act 1947 centralised responsibility in the hands of counties and county boroughs and introduced a comprehensive system for the control of development.

The police and the fire brigade provide further examples of the transfer of functions to fewer and larger units of operation. After the Police Act 1946 the remaining non-county borough forces were absorbed into the county police; in the 1960s the centralisation process continued with the amalgamation of county and county borough forces. Counties became the fire authority under the Fire Brigades Act 1947.

In recent years local authorities have done much to extend leisure facilities. There has been a burgeoning of swimming pools, sports centres and arts centres. Fees are charged to those who use the facilities but the revenue rarely covers the cost; so a subsidy from the rates becomes essential. In addition, local authorities provide financial aid for a wide variety of voluntary organisations which provide recreational and cultural activities. There is no doubt that such expenditure widens the opportunities available to the community. It can also be highly controversial. No statutory requirement exists to use money in this way; the decision to spend is entirely a matter for local discretion and is a ready target for those who seek to cut back expenditure. Some major projects of this kind are defended on the ground that they bring additional business to a town; the Brighton conference centre is a leading example.

It must be noted that local authorities are not merely executive agencies. They exist not only to carry out duties but also to express opinions. This representative function has two forms. Local authorities can urge other public bodies to carry out policies which will be of local advantage. Government departments can be pressed to encourage industrial development in a particular area: Regional Traffic Commissioners can be asked to stop proposed fare increases on the buses. The second aspect of this representational activity is for one local authority to ask another, usually a larger authority, to do something. Counties receive many requests from districts. The executive tasks of a parish are small, but a parish council may be very active in pressing local problems on district or county councils.

THE ALLOCATION OF DUTIES

Beyond the question what powers local authorities should have, there lies the issue, what sort of authority is suitable to carry out any particular task? So when a fresh activity is being introduced into local government one asks whether it should be given to top-tier or second-tier councils; the same problem arises when a service is being extended. Any discussion of a major reorganisation of local government structure will include arguments about the size of local authorities, and size is more often considered in the context of population rather than acreage.

There has been constant pressure to eliminate the smallest and weakest councils. Many urban and rural districts disappeared during the county reviews of the 1930s; the total of urban districts was reduced from 786 to 573 while rural districts fell from 650 to 477. In the postwar debate about local government reform much weight was placed on the idea that small authorities were incapable of doing their job properly. The smallest county was Rutland with a population around 25,000; how could such a county provide a full education service and a wide range of residential care for those in need, including the young, the aged and the handicapped?

Of course, it was not possible. For many purposes Rutland had to rely on purchasing facilities from adjacent authorities. Such arrangements must be cumbersome and hard to justify. But the argument for larger units does not stay merely with the proposition that more population and rateable value are needed to provide specialised services; the issue is not the level at which provision can be made, but the level at which greatest efficiency is achieved. Great stress is laid upon economics of scale. Big is beautiful. The bigger the organisation, the more readily it can afford specialised equipment, buildings and staff. The larger body can offer better opportunities for promotion. A more favourable career structure will attract better quality staff and improve motivation. The ability to use professional expertise and modern technology, especially computers, must improve the range, competence and cost-effectiveness of the services provided. Further, it is claimed that the public expects a fairly uniform standard of service throughout the country, especially as local government is heavily subsidised by the national Exchequer. A smaller number of authorities facilitates uniformity. Such arguments are familiar, if not necessarily wholly justified.

The case for fewer and bigger local authorities was well set out in the evidence presented by government departments to the Redcliffe-Maud Commission on Local Government. All departments favoured larger units of local government in the interests of efficiency and uniformity. No doubt they felt that fewer local authorities would be easier to supervise. The Ministry of Transport wished for thirty to forty major transport authorities to replace the then 823 highway authorities and 1,190 parking authorities. Indeed, all departments favoured thirty to forty major authorities. How did these magic figures occur separately to so many minds? Within the overall figure of thirty to forty authorities there was some variation of approach. Education sought a population of 500,000 with a minimum of 300,000, but Health was prepared to go down to 200,000. There was also difference about the need for second-tier authorities: Housing and Local Government accepted the need for a second tier, the Treasury assumed all-purpose authorities while Transport was unsure – 'there is no advantage in creating lower-tier authorities in areas which could be adequately governed at first-tier level'.

The departmental view that education authorities required a population of 500,000 implied that the London boroughs were far too small to be effective education authorities. This was curious since these authorities were created as recently as 1963, and minimum sizes of authority are generally thought of as being *higher* in densely populated areas. Further, the evidence submitted by the inspectorate in the Department of Education and Science indicated that the quality of service suffered where the population of an LEA was below 200,000: however, the inspectors judged authorities in the 200–250,000 bracket to be superior to those in the 300–400,000 bracket and equal to those in the 400–500,000 range. Thus the 500,000 standard and absolute minimum of 300,000 suggested by the Department were open to objection.

The Royal Commission's report stimulated arguments against big units. Authorities covering large areas would be inconvenient for the public and also for councillors who would have to travel further to attend council and committee meetings. Local government would become less accessible and more remote. The consequent large reduction in the number of councillors would mean that local administration was less subject to detailed scrutiny by elected representatives. The cause of democracy would suffer. At a more sophisticated level, it was urged that the sense of commitment and individual responsibility suffered in larger organisations.

This general train of thought was influential in maintaining the system of two-tier local government. In particular it helped to strengthen the role of metropolitan districts as it was felt that metropolitan counties would be too large for the provision of personal services. Nevertheless an expensive service like education does require substantial financial resources and a minimum population around 200,000 was deemed essential for a local education authority. Specialised services, required by few people or which demand the use of highly skilled staff in short supply, go to authorities with substantial population. The top tier also has responsibility for functions which are felt to demand most uniformity or perhaps greater control by central government: the police are an obvious example. The second-tier authorities are responsible for services when local knowledge and responsiveness to local needs are held to be of paramount importance. Which of these criteria apply most forcibly to any particular local function must be a matter of opinion. Spokesmen for counties and districts argued these issues at length during the protracted discussions on local government reform.

The following paragraphs explain in general terms the distribution of functions under the terms of the Local Government Act 1972. Formal lists of functions are given in Appendix B. However, some preliminary points should be noted. Powers are not uniform among each category of local authorities because of provisions in private Bills. There are also minor variations in Wales. Nor are duties uniform as between local authorities in the same sub-group because the 1972 Act gives a general power to authorities to arrange for another local authority to carry out specified duties on an agency basis. This power of transfer is subject to exceptions – the administration of education and the social services, the right to levy a rate, to raise a loan and, curiously, functions under the Diseases of Animals Act 1850.

Non-metropolitan counties are responsible for education, libraries and social services, but not so the metropolitan counties. The financial effect is dramatic. The former account for 85 per cent of expenditure in their areas, the latter for only 20 per cent. It follows that the second tier in the metropolitan areas is significantly more important. London follows the metropolitan pattern save that education in the inner London area is controlled by a committee of the GLC representing the inner London boroughs. Wales follows the non-metropolitan pattern. Another distinction is that metropolitan counties are passenger transport authorities: elsewhere this function is performed, if at all, by districts. However, all counties are responsible for promoting public transport policy in conjunction with bus operators and British Rail.

All counties are police and fire brigade authorities. (In London the Metropolitan Police are the direct responsibility of the Home Secretary.) Consumer protection, including the inspection of weights and measures, food and drugs, is another general field of county activity except in London and sometimes in Wales. Minor items on the list are road safety and the provision of small holdings. Some counties have special duties in connection with National Parks.

Other functions are shared between counties and districts, notably planning and highways. Counties prepare structure plans which determine the broad strategy of development for their areas: districts prepare local plans which set out more precisely the detailed implementation of county policy. Districts also decide whether to grant development permission. Districts issue enforcement orders and revocations of planning permission. Both counties and districts have powers in relation to town development. Another example of shared responsibility relates to abandoned motor vehicles; districts remove them but counties destroy them. This is a particular application of the general principle that districts collect refuse but counties destroy it. Counties are the major highway authorities and are responsible for road maintenance. Districts can claim to maintain unclassified roads in urban areas, that is, the territory of former boroughs and urban districts: this work is carried out at county expense and subject to county cost control. Counties are responsible for local traffic orders and control of parking but districts have concurrent powers, with county consent, to provide off-street car parks. Other concurrent powers relate to recreation and leisure facilities, swimming baths, open spaces and entertainments, aerodromes and action in natural emergencies.

District functions also cover environmental and public health services, including building regulations, clean air, drainage and inspection of offices, shops and factories. Housing is perhaps the most important duty. Counties, except in Wales, have reserve housing powers but these can be used only on the request of a district council. Districts collect the rates. They can operate buses where local powers existed before 1972; in addition they can subsidise services and provide travel concessions. They can provide allotments, markets and civic restaurants, and are responsible for coast protection.

Districts are licensing authorities for theatres, cinemas, night refreshment houses and many other purposes. Welsh districts have an additional significance for they constitute the areas for holding septennial referenda to determine whether alcohol should be on public sale on Sunday in licensed premises.

The minor local authorities, the towns, parishes and communities should not be forgotten. Their powers are optional and of limited importance. They include provision and maintenance of allotments, burial grounds, public clocks, footpaths, bus shelters, recreation grounds, street lighting and war memorials. In addition they have various powers in relation to charities and common or parish land. But a major part of the business of the minor authorities is to represent local opinion to other local authorities and public bodies. It follows that parish and community councils can and do discuss many items which fall outside the scope of their executive duties. In particular they can claim to be consulted on local planning applications. There is no doubt that a vigorous parish or community council can play a valuable role in protecting the rural environment and it provides an opportunity, sadly lacking in the wards of boroughs, to ventilate local opinion.

Overall, the 1972 Act marked a further stage in the process of making local government less local. It reduced the number of top-tier county level authorities to less than 40 per cent of the previous total. As metropolitan districts retain education and social services, the cut in the number of authorities responsible for these functions was not quite so severe.

To be fair, the 1972 Act did provide for some decentralisation. Previously many districts had exercised some delegated powers in relation to town and country planning but the Act gave them control over planning questions that did not affect county policy. In 1980 the position of the districts was further strengthened as they gained virtually complete control over development applications. In view of the growing public interest in planning matters, this is a major advance for district councils. Some licensing duties have also been handed down from counties to districts, and, as noted above, there is the possibility of agency arrangements to carry out county duties.

In spite of some recent moves towards decentralisation the dominant tendency in public administration is the other way. While some functions have been moved from second-tier to top-tier local authorities, others have been taken away altogether from local government. This started with the creation of Regional Traffic Commissioners in 1930 and the loss to them of the power to license road passenger services. Relief of the unemployed went to the Unemployment Assistance Board in 1934. In the postwar period gas and electricity undertakings were nationalised and hospitals were taken over by regional boards. At the same time the valuation of property for the purpose of rating was transferred to the Inland Revenue. A further serious loss of powers took place in 1974 when the personal health services, water supply and sewerage passed on to regional authorities.

For a century after the reform of the poor law in 1834 local authorities enjoyed a steady growth of their responsibilities. In the postwar period while some further powers have been obtained, others have been taken away. Increasingly, the losses outweigh the gains. Local government is in competition with other types of public body. It faces the challenge of rival institutions.

How can this change of fortune be explained? There were two main reasons for the burgeoning of local government after 1834. The agreement that public provision of services should be allowed to develop was a hesitant agreement, for this period was the heyday of individualistic doctrines. The sentiment that government of any kind is but a necessary evil leads to the supposition that local government is a lesser evil than national government because it is more susceptible to public control. The great indignation aroused by the attempts of national government to influence local affairs in the Chadwick period is eloquent proof of the force of this attitude. The second reason can be stated quite simply – local government had no competitors. The highly competent Civil Service of today evolved very slowly in the latter part of the nineteenth century. Even in the early years of this century the organisational resources of government departments were rudimentary except for tax collection. Public corporations did not appear until the 1920s. Thus the administrative capacity of local authorities, however deficient it may have been by modern standards, held a dominating position.

All this has now changed. Collectivism is in fashion rather than individualism: technical requirements demand large-scale production to achieve economies of scale: the need for efficiency and uniformity is held to require fewer and bigger units of organisation. Take the particular example of the health service. There was an undeniable case for bringing together under one management the three original sections of the National Health Service – the personal health services provided by local authorities, the hospitals and the various individual practitioners. Why could they not be unified within the context of a democratically controlled local government system? The traditional objection, that local authority areas are unsuitable, might have been met if the needs of the health service had been taken into account when local government areas were reshaped in 1972. However, there were three other powerful factors working against the claims of local government. The professional interests involved, particularly the doctors, feared the loss of freedom if they were subject to the direction of local councillors. Local authorities have inadequate financial resources to provide all health services; they would require either new powers to tax or massive additional grants from the central government. And if national government money is being spent, then ministers like to be able to control how it is done. There is no doubt that the reluctance of many local authorities to provide family planning facilities has aroused irritation in Whitehall.

Thus local government is on the defensive. In any discussion about how a new service should be provided, or how some existing service could be reformed, the case for local government no longer dominates; on the contrary, it is increasingly difficult to sustain.

Chapter 4

POLITICS AND PERSONNEL

A local authority, like any other piece of state mechanism, is governed by both law and practice. The conventions that develop within the formal structure of a local authority have a great effect on the way in which business is carried through and how decisions are made. No systematic description of the arrangements is possible since they vary between each authority. There is, however, one dominating factor – the extent to which a council is influenced by the political loyalties of elected members. The importance of political parties in framing the conventions of public life can scarely be exaggerated. The work of a local authority is based on the interrelationships of officials and elected representatives working together through a committee system. Especially in urban areas the outcome is substantially affected by party activity. To ignore the effect of politics on local government is unrealistic and misleading: a broad description of the political setting must be given before we move on to consider the respective roles of officers and councillors.

THE IMPACT OF POLITICS

It is often argued that politics should have no place in local government. Certainly there are some grounds for this view. Where elections are held on a party basis, no candidate other than those sponsored by a party has a real chance of success. Where one party is dominant in a particular ward or district, nomination by that party is tantamount to election to the local council, for electors become accustomed to voting on party lines and do not know, or do not care about, the qualities of the individual candidate. Attachment to a political party thus becomes an essential pre-condition of election to a local council; in so far as this limits the field of recruitment, the quality of elected members may be reduced. There must be many men and women of high ability who would be willing to serve on local authorities but who are unwilling to give unswerving support to a party or who happen to belong to a political minority in their own locality. The other main causes of complaint are that where councillors organise themselves into political groups, decisions are taken by the majority group in private meetings, and that politics are allowed to affect details of local administration which are quite beyond the normal bounds of party controversy.

Equally, however, a strong case can be made in favour of party politics. Party activity does much to increase interest in local elections: party conflict tends to reduce the number of unopposed elections, and to raise the proportion of the electorate who vote in contested elections. Further, if a candidate is returned without a party label, it does not follow that he has no political affiliations but merely that he has not declared any he may have. To argue that politics should be taken out of local government is, in part, to misunderstand the nature of politics. In a democracy we argue freely about the proper aims and methods of public policy. This is political discussion. Inevitably, the major questions which confront local authorities, education, housing, planning, raise issues which are political in nature and attract the attention of political organisations. The idea that these matters should be left to 'the best man for the job' is fanciful since one cannot decide who is the best man unless the opinions of candidates are revealed. The charge that party groups should not have private 'caucus' meetings to settle policy is countered by showing that this is analogous to what happens in our national government; no one suggests it is wrong for Conservative and Labour MPs to hold separate private gatherings or that party leaders should not meet in conditions of secrecy at Cabinet or 'Shadow' Cabinet meetings. Party organisation in a democracy is essential for opinions to be organised into broad streams. The group or party representing the dominant stream of opinion becomes responsible for the conduct of public affairs for a limited time, and may be displaced from power at a subsequent election if it displeases the voters. It follows that where the business of a local authority is conducted on a party basis it is more likely to be planned and consistent than if it depends on unorganised and changing views of individual councillors.

Whatever view one takes of these theoretical considerations, it is vital to recognise that the impact of politics on local government is growing steadily. Even in rural areas, most local elections are now fought on a party basis. What does vary, however, and what is most difficult to determine, is how far party organisation affects the actual working of a local council. The variety of local arrangements is best illustrated by the description of extremes. In some councils, party loyalty matters little; members may be elected on a party basis but, once elected, tend to act as individuals; committee chairmen are chosen irrespective of politics and no group meetings are held. This arrangement is becoming increasingly scarce. At the other extreme, party governs everything important. The majority group meets to determine policy on major issues; it secures a majority on all committees; it nominates the chairmen and vice-chairmen of all committees; the parties require complete obedience from their members, and any councillor who refuses to support a party decision is expelled from the group and will not get party support at the next election. Such extensive party influence is common among the larger authorities and in areas dominated by the Labour Party. There are still some authorities, especially among district councils, which fall in between the patterns defined above; party groups meet irregularly and voting is not always dominated by the concept of party loyalty. And sometimes where the party spirit is strong, the effect of politics is restrained because no one group has an overall majority of seats.

Against this background of an uneven degree of party activity, the work of elected members, officers and committees continues. Where the party element is strong, the ability of elected members to speak their minds freely in public is curtailed. On major issues the only free discussion may take place in the privacy of the party meeting where party policy is decided, if necessary by a vote. An elected member who finds himself in a minority among party colleagues is required to bow to the necessity of political unity and vote against his opinion at committee and council meetings. Where strict party discipline operates, it follows that the policy adopted need not represent the will of the majority, but only the will of the majority of the majority – which may well be a minority of the whole.

There is another possible source of tension. Conflict may develop between a local party organisation and their councillors. Such strife is most likely in the Labour Party. Local Labour parties may argue that they alone decide local policy and present a programme to the local electors. It is then the task of Labour councillors, if the party wins a majority, to put the programme into practice. There can be disputes over interpretation, timing and what is practicable in the current economic circumstances. Councillors may feel inhibited by difficulties that local party activists would ignore. Councillors may also claim that they are responsible to the whole electorate and not merely to the party faithful who attend local branch meetings. All these issues are related to a wider debate in the Labour Party about the nature of representative democracy. Is anyone elected as an MP or a councillor entitled to use individual judgement, or should he submit to instructions from the party organisation which gave him the party nomination, without which he would not have been elected? Are those elected with a party label, representatives or delegates from the party? The argument here is not about an individual straying from the party line: it is whether a party group of elected representatives should submit to instructions from outside.

Councillors obeying such instructions could incur, in extreme cases, severe financial penalties imposed by a court at the behest of the district auditor. It is not surprising that Labour councillors, while willing to accept the authority of their own group on the council, are far less ready to accept edicts from the local party organisation. Further, the officers will have less influence on the direction of local affairs if party considerations govern policy and major decisions are taken at private meetings which officers do not attend. Even so, the picture must not be exaggerated. However intense party activity may be, a mass of minor matters remain to be settled by committee debate and by consulation between chief officers and committee chairmen.

One other aspect of party intervention at local elections demands comment. Increasingly the electors vote not upon local questions but depending on their view of national events. What the government does is felt to be more important than what the council does. Since ministers are often unpopular, their supporters do badly at local elections. The pendulum swings and local majorities are displaced because of dissatisfaction with the Cabinet. Councillors are defeated irrespective of their own part in local affairs. The danger emerges that local government ceases to be accountable for its actions, since it is not judged on its actions. Restraints of democratic responsibility can be undermined. Party politics cannot be blamed for this situation for parties do not control the behaviour of voters: it is not the fault of parties if electors choose to ignore local issues. Indeed, such preference may be rational. If people feel more affected, or even threatened, by national policies than by local affairs, then it is sensible for them to use any opportunity that occurs to protest against the government in the hope that ministers will heed the evidence of popular discontent and respond accordingly.

COUNCILLORS

About 24,000 councillors are elected to the county, district and borough councils in England and Wales. What kind of people are they? The latest survey was undertaken in 1976 for the Committee on the Remuneration of Councillors. It showed that half the councillors were below the age of 55 but only a quarter were below 45. Only 17 per cent were women. Certain occupations predominated, notably employers, managers, professional workers and farmers; no doubt such people can most easily arrange to be free to attend council meetings. Sixteen per cent of councillors had retired. Half had gained qualifications arising from higher education; this proportion is likely to increase since younger councillors have more qualifications than their older colleagues. Seventy-six per cent were owner-occupiers; 16 per cent were council tenants. The average earnings of a councillor appeared to be rather above the average for the whole population, but this information is less reliable because some councillors failed to reveal their income. It is clear that those chosen to represent us do not form a typical cross-section of society. Equally, their social composition is too mixed for them to constitute anything approaching a distinct elite.

Newly elected councillors can often experience acute frustration. On many authorities the individual councillor can do nothing except through the party group, and the group may not welcome initiatives from backbenchers. Council and committee procedure appears complex to the uninitiated. And if you do not know the rules of the game, you will not be able to play it very successfully. The sacrifice of time is substantial. The task is not simply to attend a variety of meetings but to prepare for them. Agenda papers and reports must be studied if a worthwhile contribution to a policy discussion is to be made. How far councillors really master the voluminous material sent to them is a matter of doubt: those who have some experience of management necessarily have an advantage. Some councillors learn the system quicker than others; some will be permanently confused or unaware of its intricacies, particularly in regard to finance. Meanwhile they suffer a loss of privacy, possibly damage to family life and very often a financial sacrifice. An employer may tolerate an employee who becomes a councillor but he is less likely to promote him or her.

Especially in urban areas, the turnover of councillors can be rather high. Partly this is due to the behaviour of the voters and the swings of party fortune: partly it is because councillors do not seek re-nomination. Experience of public life breeds disenchantment, often because of a feeling that it is so difficult to get anything done.

The number of people a councillor attempts to represent varies with the status of the authority and the nature of the area. A member of the Greater London Council represents about 80,000 people. A member of a large non-metropolitan county represents at least 12,000 people. A district councillor is likely to represent on average about 2,000 people. Areas which have third-tier authorities also enjoy supplementary representation through parish or community councillors. Representation is strongest, in constitutional terms, when population is relatively sparse.

How far is it possible for a councillor to keep in touch with public opinion? With few exceptions a councillor is not a full-time politician. His or her job may tend to isolate them from the community. A small shop keeper will meet a cross-section of the population every day – but most people do not. In some urban areas councillors hold 'surgeries' to deal with individual problems. Councillors meet a few party supporters at party meetings. On particular issues, they can be lobbied by pressure groups. County and district councillors for rural areas can use parish authorities as a focus of local opinion. But these communication links are partial and spasmodic. It is difficult to resist the conclusion that the councillor is only a little less isolated than everyone else. The strongest influence upon him is a party group of like-minded councillors; beyond that he follows his own inclination.

The reduction in the number of councillors implies that those who remain have even heavier duties. If councillors have heavy responsibilities – should they be paid? The Local Government Act 1948 entitled members of local authorities to claim for loss of earnings on the basis of a somewhat niggardly scale, but this did not constitute payment. It was compensation rather than remuneration, a compromise that avoided paying a salary. The arguments against changing the tradition of honorary public service in local government were formidable. There was no wide demand that it should be altered. Indeed, the Social Survey report to the Maud Committee showed that both councillors and ex-councillors are generally hostile to the idea: the report also showed that lack of time rather than financial reasons was the main barrier to the recruitment of young, well-educated councillors. Payment introduces a new and unpleasant question of motivation: all council candidates are open to the sneer that they wish to be elected to get easy money. Were this type of attitude to become prevalent, it is probable that many people would be deterred from standing and some present councillors might drop out. Payment also increases the burden on the local rate and is thus unlikely to be popular with ratepayers. There is also a difficult question about how much should be paid. If the sums involved are substantial and designed to attract people of ability, the operation must be costly and there can be no guarantee that people of the requisite calibre will come forward – or that they will be elected. Large payments could well attract the wrong sort of person to council work. On the other hand, if the amounts offered are too small, councils may still be dominated by retired persons or those with inadequate ability and experience.

The case for making payments is far stronger. Unless some financial recompense is available for councillors, many people who must spend the greater part of their time earning a living are perforce unable to offer their services and the field of recruitment will be limited to housewives, retired people, the self-employed and those fortunate enough to have sympathetic employers willing to release them for local government work. Elected representatives naturally spend varying amounts of time on council work; their burden will depend on their personal inclinations, the size of the authority and their status within it. Leading councillors in the larger authorities, including the chairmen of major committees, already devote a great deal of time each week to public service. For some these duties will become virtually a full-time occupation. Why should we expect all this effort without significant financial cost to the community? If our councillors are to fairly represent all sections of the community, particularly if we want younger and able councillors, payment must be made.

The Local Government Act 1972 authorised the government to fix a maximum daily rate that can be paid to councillors for attending to council business. Sums paid were modest; *pro rata* they were no more than the pay of junior local government officers. All councillors received the same rate of payment, but the amounts received by individuals varied with the time spent on council business. This attendance allowance was taxable. Co-opted members of local authority committees who were not elected councillors got no attendance payment but could claim an allowance for financial loss that was not taxable. These provisions in the 1972 Act recognised that councillors are likely to suffer financially as a result of their public service, but it was widely held that the payments allowed were too small to meet the situation.

The Callaghan government appointed a committee under the chairmanship of Mr Derek Robinson to review the problem. Its report (Cmnd 7010) published in 1977 found that many councillors did suffer financially from their public service. The committee felt this should be remedied. Accordingly, it proposed that councillors receive a basic sum of £1,000 which would be taxable, together with travel and subsistence allowances. Further, councillors who could show they suffered financial loss from 'approved duties' should be entitled to receive further sums as compensation, the amount of which would be adjusted in accordance with the marginal tax rate of each individual. Another proposal that councillors who have greater responsibilities, that is, the chairmen of major committees, should get extra payment, is discussed in the following section.

The Thatcher government was not wholly unsympathetic to councillors but it was determined to restrain public expenditure. So the idea of a basic salary was rejected. However, the Local Government, Planning and Land Act 1980 did offer councillors an option between the attendance allowance and the financial loss allowance; the choice may benefit some councillors depending upon their individual position relating to income tax. Also the 1980 Act allows the levels of both types of allowance to be reviewed annually, so there is some prospect that they will keep pace with inflation. Of course, councillors and co-opted members of local authority committees can claim for travelling and subsistence expenses on an approved scale when engaged on council business. It is a matter for each education authority to decide whether to pay such expenses to school governors. Parish and community councillors receive no payment of any kind for duties carried out within the area of their own council. Finally, a local authority can insure its members against death or injury while engaged on council business.

There are many qualifications governing candidature at local elections. A councillor must be 21 years of age and a British subject. He must also be on the register of electors for the authority concerned, unless during the twelve months prior to the election he had been resident in the area, or it has been his principal place of work, or he has been the owner or tenant of land or buildings within it. For a parish or community councillor the residence qualification is more flexible: he must have lived within 3 miles of the area during the preceding year. People who satisfy these conditions may still be disqualified by any one of the following rules. An employee of a local authority cannot be an elected member of it. So a teacher employed by a metropolitan district can serve on the county council: a teacher employed for a county council can serve on his district council. Bankruptcy is a disqualification, so is a surcharge of £500 by the district auditor within five years of the election. Those convicted of corrupt practices at elections are barred as well as those convicted for any offence within the last five years for which the penalty imposed was imprisonment for three months or more without the option of a fine. Further, a councillor who is absent from council meetings for six months will vacate his seat unless the authority approves his reason for absence.

The barrier against local authority staff does limit the availability of prospective councillors. No doubt the disqualification is imposed because it is felt that an employee should not join his employing body, as this would produce a conflict of interest. Clearly, it would be inappropriate for an administrative officer to be elected to the council which it is his duty to advise and assist. Whether the ban should extend to all employees, in particular to manual workers, is a matter for argument. They would have to be prohibited from speaking or voting on any resolution affecting their own remuneration or conditions of service. Subject to this safeguard why should a manual worker not be eligible for election? There does seem an element of hypocrisy in a system which disqualifies a dustman from election to his district council because of some alleged conflict of interest but which does not take similar precautions in relation to estate agents, building contractors and surveyors. However, the Redcliffe-Maud Committee on Conduct in Local Government recommended firmly that present restriction on local authority staff should remain unaltered.

Perhaps the most intractable constitutional problem affecting councillors is the relationship between their public duties and their business interests. The law on this topic is now governed by section 94 of the Local Government Act 1972. In essence, the position is that a councillor who has a financial interest in any contract or other matter coming before his authority must disclose his interest and not vote or participate in discussion thereon. Failure to observe this rule renders the defaulter liable to a fine not exceeding £200 for each offence: any such prosecution must be initiated by the Director of Public Prosecutions. The details of the law are complex. Interests of a spouse are included in the ban provided the marriage partners are living together. Membership of a partnership or company is also included. But the disability is removed wherever an interest is so remote that it cannot reasonably be regarded as likely to influence a councillor's conduct. And shareholdings in a company do not disqualify where the nominal amount is below £1,000 or below one-hundredth of the issued share capital of the company, whichever is less. A councillor can make a general statement of his interests in writing to be available for inspection by other councillors; this will obviate the need for a specific declaration of interest on each item that is linked to his business concerns. Another escape route is that the secretary of state can remove this disability from a council on any particular occasion when he feels the public interest so requires, perhaps because so many councillors would otherwise be disqualified. A district council has a similar power of dispensation in relation to a parish council.

Section 94 is decreasingly relevant to the situation. The original legislation, section 76 of the Local Government Act 1933, was designed to ensure that there should be no improper influence exercised by businessmen who might have contracts with their local authority. Today the threat to probity in local government is quite different. It is that elected members may use 'inside' information about probable future policy in relation to land use for their private advantage. If a member knows that his authority is likely to take certain action which will affect property values, he may make shrewd bargains before the intentions of the authority reach the stage of formal decisions and become public knowledge. Such behaviour is beyond the scope of section 94. The problem is not that abuse is widespread but rather the virtual impossibility of formulating legislation that would effectively prevent it. To extend to local government some form of Official Secrets Act is at present beyond the bounds of possibility: it would certainly discourage recruitment of councillors. Many authorities have a Standing Order which decrees that committee business shall be treated as confidential until it is communicated to the council or the press, but such an instruction cannot be a watertight safeguard against abuse. A council could decide to exclude from its planning committee any member with interest in business or property; the individual application of such a rule could be very unpleasant, it would deprive the planning committee of useful experience and would not necessarily stop the circulation of valuable information. The best safeguards seem to be the consciences of elected members and the pressure of public opinion.

There is no doubt that authoritarian party structures have created opportunities for corruption as they have helped local leaders to evade criticism and detection. Growing concern at such behaviour, especially after the various cases connected with the architect John Poulson, led to the appointment of a committee to inquire into standards of conduct in local government. The chairman was Lord Redcliffe-Maud. The report, published in 1974, concluded that local government was essentially honest but that corruption spreads unless it is stopped. So a number of additional precautions were proposed. The committee recommended that the law on disclosure of interests be made tougher. Councillors should be required to disclose an interest orally and thereafter withdraw from the meeting while the relevant item was under discussion unless a dispensation had been received from the secretary of state. Councillors should also be required to enter certain interests on a public register. A councillor should not be chairman of a committee whose affairs are linked to his personal interests; sometimes councillors should not even be members. The use of information received through membership of a local authority for private gain should be a criminal offence. The report argued that 'openness' in local administration was a valuable safeguard. It also recommended that the associations of local authorities draw up a national code of conduct for all councillors; this would define standards and have an important persuasive force.

The discussion of pecuniary interests raises the question of motive. Why do people continue to serve for long periods on local authorities? No authoritative answer to this question is possible. If elected members are asked why they serve, their replies will be highly subjective. Obviously they may be fired by political enthusiasm or be attracted by whatever prestige is associated with the word 'councillor'. It is probably true that most elected members feel that they are doing something useful for the community. A council and its committees become a sort of informal club which the retired members, in particular, find attractive. It is also possible that a few people join local councils out of the hope that financial advantage will be derived therefrom: certainly this is sometimes believed to be so by the general public. Should the idea spread that councillors are in local government for what they can get out of it, persons jealous of their reputation will avoid membership of local authorities. The 'club' would cease to be an attractive one. Here the problem is put bluntly, not because of any immediate prospect that this situation will occur but because it is a danger not to be overlooked. The maintenance of probity in local government is of the utmost importance from every point of view.

LEADERS, CHAIRMEN AND MAYORS

In theory, all councillors have equal status and an equal right to influence the business of their local authority. In practice, councillors are by no means equal to each other. Party groups elect leaders. The leader of the majority group is often known as the leader of the council – in effect a local Prime Minister. He (or she) may achieve a position of dominance. Chairmen of major committees can attain a key role in the work of a particular department of a local authority. Councillors who have not been chosen for such positions, in parliamentary terms the backbenchers, necessarily have much less influence. A variety of factors help the ruling elite to keep their place. They are usually more experienced than their critics; they spend more time on council business and are better informed; above all, they draw support from the conventions imposed by party loyalty. Where a council is run on strict party lines, backbenchers will not be expected to challenge their own party's policy at formal council and committee meetings. Dissent has to be restricted to private party meetings. Here a determined chairman may be able to ride roughshod over any opponents, especially as the time available for these meetings may be short. There have been some behind-the-scenes rows about how far detailed information should be made available to backbench members of a majority group. They may be told that if they demand information, it must be made available equally to their political opponents, the councillors in the minority group(s). If the material is damaging then it will be used to harass the majority and can even have repercussions at local elections. So where party machines are tightly organised, a backbench councillor can feel as far away from the seats of power as a backbench MP. In these circumstances the backbencher has a major chance to influence policy only when the group leadership is under attack at a private caucas gathering: here his vote can matter.

Of course, the concept of the 'city boss' is not entirely new. Joseph Chamberlain was a dominant figure in Birmingham in the 1870s. In the early years of this century Alderman Salvidge had enormous sway in Liverpool as did Sir Sidney Kimber in Southampton. But these men depended on personality rather than strict party discipline.

The question of payments for councillors, discussed in the previous section, becomes even more acute in the case of those exercising leadership. These people will be spending more time on council work. Many will also be involved in the activities of the associations of local authorities. At this stage local government becomes, or should become, virtually a full-time occupation. It is arguable that local authorities would be more efficient if leaders and chairmen could spend more time studying background material about the important decisions that must be made. A large majority of those who have to earn a living could not adjust to a schedule of this kind without severe financial loss. How can this problem be solved? Should those who have exceptional responsibilities receive exceptional payment?

The Robinson Committee felt it was essential that extra pay should be available. It recommended that up to one-tenth of the councillors on a local authority, subject to a maximum of eight, should get more money. So the special responsibilities of the leader, the mayor or chairman and up to six committee chairmen could be recognised. The amount paid should depend on the size of the authority: the smallest authorities below 50,000 population should pay an extra £750, on top of the £1,000 that would go to all councillors, while at the other extreme where population exceeded 400,000, the extra pay should be £3,000. The Robinson Report appeared in 1977 so today the sums paid would have to be much higher to provide the real return envisaged in the report.

The 1980 Act authorised extra payments for councillors with special responsibilities. Each county and district council is permitted, but not required, to provide such reimbursement. Government regulations fix the maximum amount to be distributed; the sum depends on the size and status of an authority. No one may receive more than one-third of the money available for distribution by his council and this restriction is subject to a further maximum of £4,000. Such payment is an addition to the attendance allowance or financial loss allowance. Even so, the income available to a full-time councillor is significantly below salaries paid to those in professional and managerial occupations. Indeed, skilled workers could be out of pocket. Job security for elected councillors is poor. Electors may be fickle or a party caucus may decide to change its leaders. Anyone in a secure well-paid post would be unwise to change it for a career as a full-time councillor. It is probable that the scheme of responsibility payments has not solved the problem of improving the quality of council leadership.

Meanwhile, various problems may arise. Should a minority group benefit? Elections for party leader and committee chairmen may arouse greater tension and jealousy. Will there be a tendency to choose those who are felt to have greater need of the extra money? Will the public understand that not all councillors get the extra pay? The backbench councillor may be irked by his lack of influence; he will be even more irritated if he finds that he is generally believed to be getting a considerable salary. And anyone who stands for election, especially to a large authority, might be open to the charge of seeking to make money from political and public service. The extra payments are made more controversial by the current atmosphere about public expenditure. In view of these varied considerations, it is unsurprising that many authorities have not yet started to make them.

The first business at the annual meeting of a local authority is to elect the chairman. A chairman may be the most influential member of his council, keeping in regular touch with senior officials about policy developments and giving general direction to affairs. Alternatively, at least during his year of office, he may stand aside from controversial matters and perceive his main duty to be the impartial control of council meetings. Where party organisation is strong the latter model is likely to be adopted. Local traditions depend upon the political situation. The method of filling the office is a good guide to how it is used. If a new chairman is elected each year, possibly on the basis of seniority or as a result of agreement between political groups, then he is likely to exercise minimum influence. But if a chairman is re-elected time and time again, one suspects that he is an important force in council affairs.

The essential difference between a mayor and a chairman is that the latter does not have such an intense social programme. District and county chairmen will make some appearances on public occasions and may wear a chain of office, but their status is not so high. Yet a mayor has dignity rather than power. In some other countries the title 'mayor' describes an official who has substantial personal responsibilities for the proper conduct of local administration. The French *maire* is in this position. In the United States the situation is complicated because there are many forms of town government and the traditional mayor and council pattern has often been replaced by other systems thought to be more efficient or to provide firmer safeguards against corruption, but where the mayor survives he generally has substantial personal responsibilities, analogous to those of the President in relation to the federal government. The British mayor has a quite different position. His executive tasks are minimal. His main formal duty is to preside at council meetings and ensure that these are conducted properly in accordance with the rules of council procedure. But mayors are always busy people. They are expected to undertake a formidable programme of appearances at various public occasions, to entertain distinguished visitors who come to their borough, to attend civic, cultural and charitable events, school speechdays and to visit local hospitals, especially on Christmas Day. This whirl of social activity is punctuated by speeches of welcome and votes of thanks. The mayor becomes the embodiment of the community of the borough. By statute he has precedence over all other persons save a direct representative of the Crown such as the Lord-Lieutenant of the county. The mayoralty is held in deep respect, but the respect belongs to the office and not to the man who holds it. This respect demands that the mayor abstain from controversial activities – in the same way as the Speaker of the House of Commons: the general pattern is that the mayor takes no part in political events during his period of office. It follows that he does not concern himself with the details of local administration. He does not direct or supervise borough officers. If important decisions have to be taken between committee meetings, the responsibility falls on the appropriate committee chairman rather than the mayor. The normal position is that the mayor will exercise initiative only in unusual circumstances and then in a non-controversial manner. Thus if there is a local disaster the mayor may open a relief fund; by acting in this way he is not so much providing leadership as expressing the conscience of the community. The mayoralty, then, is of much civic significance but does not bestow great influence over local affairs.

OFFICERS

The term 'local government officer' creates a mind-picture of people who work at desks in the local town hall or county hall. In fact, office-workers form but a fraction of the total employees of local authorities. Not only do local councils need the services of a large 'outdoor' manual staff concerned largely with cleansing operations and construction work, but a wide variety of skills are also required, for example, teachers, policemen, welfare workers, if all local government duties are to be carried out effectively. But the administrative and clerical staff in the local offices are at the heart of the administrative system and for this reason demand our special attention.

The days when the parish, as the most important unit of local government, could rely on the services of part-time unpaid officers are long past. Elected members have neither the time nor the range of professional expertise necessary to direct all the business of a local authority. Parliament therefore insisted that certain officers be appointed. Each county, borough and district had to have a clerk, treasurer and medical officer of health; all, except a rural district, had to have a surveyor; all, except a county, had to have a public health inspector. These legal provisions have historical significance in that they recall some unwillingness in the nineteenth century to make certain appointments, notably in relation to health, They also helped to create a uniformity in the pattern of local authority departments. Today there are fewer specific requirements in relation to the appointment of staff. The provisions mentioned above have all been swept away. However, the 1972 Act retained ten categories of officials whose employment by local authorities is compulsory: they are police officers, members of fire brigades, chief education officers, directors of social services, public analysts, agricultural analysts, weights and measures inspectors, accountants to inspect the books of pools promoters, accountants and 'experienced mechanicians' to supervise totalisator operations and the Greater London Council must appoint district surveyors. The first four items in this list are the most significant because they imply that local authorities responsible for police, fire brigades, education and social services must organise them in separate departments.

Local authorities appoint a Chief Executive with overall responsibility for the efficiency of the whole organisation. No specific qualifications are required for this post. Yet the choices made by the new councils in 1973 were very conservative; nearly always a Clerk or Deputy Clerk was chosen. A few Treasurers were appointed and Birmingham selected a Chief Planning Officer. Somerset was more adventurous and appointed a Chief Executive from outside the local government field; the sequel is mentioned below. A Chief Executive is in a strong position to exert influence. He is expected to co-ordinate the work of the separate departments and through the Management Team is kept in touch with all major issues of policy. Yet much depends on the personality of the individual. If he is respected because of his ability and other personal qualities, he will be consulted willingly by other chief officers and possibly by committee chairmen. If he is disliked or feared, his influence may be less and certainly will be achieved less happily. The most successful top administrators recognise that their main duty is to interpret the mind of their local authority rather than to mould it.

According to the Local Government Act 1972 a local authority appoints staff 'on such reasonable terms and conditions, including conditions as to remuneration' as the authority sees fit. In fact, conditions of employment are negotiated through Whitley Councils consisting of representatives of employers and employees. Often government policy has an important influence on these negotiations particularly in regard to teachers' salaries. Officers are protected from arbitrary dismissal both by their conditions of service and by the strength of trade unionism in local government. Policemen have additional safeguards. A chief constable cannot be dismissed without Home Office consent. Any policeman who is dismissed or required to resign can appeal to the Home Secretary. One other safeguard was repealed by the Local Government Act 1972 – the stipulation that the Clerk of a county council could be dismissed only with ministerial consent. In 1974 the Somerset County Council proceeded to dismiss their Chief Executive who had held office for only a few months. This incident caused great concern to SOLACE, the Society of Local Authorities' Chief Executives, which felt that some type of appeal or conciliation machinery should be established to deal with any future similar cases. However, a council cannot be expected to retain the services of a chief officer if it has no faith in his judgement or personal suitability to hold a post of great responsibility. The way out of these difficulties is to pay compensation for loss of office.

Ministerial control over appointments is also used in a few cases to prevent the selection of anyone felt to be unsuitable. The Home Secretary must approve the nomination of chief constables; there have been cases where this approval has been withheld because it was proposed to fill a vacancy by internal promotion within the local force. Similarly, he must approve the appointment of chief fire officers. The DHSS has to approve the qualifications of Directors of Social Services. Whether controls of this nature are necessary or desirable is a matter of controversy. If a local authority is regarded by Parliament as being fully capable of choosing a Chief Executive or Treasurer – why is it not capable of choosing a chief fire officer?

There has been some reduction in central controls over local staff selection. No longer does the secretary of state have to approve the appointment of a chief education officer. No longer do firemen have to be British subjects or citizens of the Republic of Ireland. But the minimum chest measurements of firemen are still prescribed by statutory instrument. The major safeguard against bad appointments is the requirement that officers in positions of responsibility should have appropriate professional qualifications. Sometimes this stipulation has a statutory basis, otherwise it is conventional or included in the schedule of agreements made through the Whitley machinery governing pay and conditions of service for local government officers. This demand for professional qualifications has certain effects on the recruitment of staff which are discussed in Chapter 7, but they are valuable in that they ensure a minimum quality of proficiency and obviate much of the possibility of corruption in making appointments. Another feature of the local government service is that promotion is obtained through moving from place to place, gaining wider experience of different conditions.

Officers of a local authority must now declare their interest in any contract involving their authority. The principle is the same as that applied to councillors. The declaration is to be in writing. Conscious failure to observe this rule renders the offender liable to a fine not exceeding £200. Whereas the prosecution of a councillor for this type of offence must be undertaken by the Director of Public Prosecutions, no such limitation is placed upon the prosecution of an official. The Redcliffe-Maud Committee on Conduct in Local Government recommended that officers should make oral disclosures of interests at meetings in the same way as councillors. It also proposed that a register of officers' interests be kept which would be open to inspection by councillors. Further, senior and professional staff should be required to agree not to take up other employment in their authority's area, without the authority's consent, for a period of two years after leaving local government service.

The central issue which affects senior local government officers is the nature of their relationship with their employing authority – how far can officers persuade elected members to accede to their views? In law, there is no problem. A council decides policy and instructs its officers to carry out its wishes; officers, as servants of the council, must obey. However, in conformity with the general law of master and servant, a local government officer cannot escape the consequences of an illegal act by pleading that he was acting under the instructions of his council. In a notable application of this principle the courts have held (*Attorney General* v. *De Winton*, 1906) that a Borough Treasurer must disobey an order from his council that calls for an illegal payment: the argument here is that a Borough Treasurer is not a mere servant of his council but has a fiduciary responsibility to the burgesses as a whole. If a Treasurer refused to carry out an instruction from his council because of doubts about its legality, it would still be open to the council, at least in theory, to dismiss their Treasurer. If ever a dispute threatened to reach this stage, public opinion would be aroused and play a large part in deciding the issue. There is no parallel ruling governing the position of a Clerk if faced with what he feels to be an illegal instruction. All that can be said is that if a Clerk wishes to secure his position against possible action by the District Auditor, he must at least ensure that the dubious instruction is given by the council as a whole and not merely by an influential member or group of members (*Re Hurle-Hobbs ex parte Riley and another*, 1944).

The inferior status of officers is symbolised by some authorities through the seating arrangements in their council chamber, for the Chief Executive sits immediately below the dais where the chairman (or mayor) presides over council meetings. This layout is extremely inconvenient whenever the chairman wishes to consult the Chief Executive. Elsewhere the Chief Executive is permitted to sit on the left hand side of the Chair; this makes it easy, perhaps too easy, for the Chief Executive to offer advice. Most officials are unhappy about proffering advice at a public council meeting except on matters of procedure where the need may be simply to remind the council of its own standing orders. They prefer to advise in the privacy of committee meetings. Necessarily the officers have a store of information which elected members would be foolish to ignore. Officers can draw upon a lifetime of professional experience and will know, or should know, not merely the legal, financial and technical complications of matters that come before committees, but the various ministerial rulings and advice as set out in Departmental Circulars and other official publications. Obviously, an official may present factual information in such a way as to lead elected members towards the policy he thinks best. But advice must always be presented tactfully. A committee resents an official who appears overbearing or impatient. A wise officer knows that a committee should always feel that it has itself made the decisions. The influence of officers tends to be greatest where an authority meets least frequently and where it is not tightly controlled by a political group: these conditions apply in some county councils. Officers view the advent of party politics in local government with mixed feelings. On the one hand, it reduces the impact they can make on policy; on the other, it probably assists continuity and certainty of policy, for once the dominant group has decided upon a course of action it is loath to retract. The party element also strengthens the need for local government officers, like civil servants, to be non-political. Where one party has controlled an authority for many years there is a danger that chief officers will be identified with the ruling party – a situation that can cause great difficulty should the party control change hands. It follows that aspiring politicians should not seek to become local administrators. Local government employees, other than teachers, rarely gain political prominence.

Chapter 5

FINANCE

A SYSTEM IN DECAY

Every benefit involves cost. Because local authorities organise a wide range of social provision, they consume a considerable fraction of the nation's resources of goods and manpower: it is now 13 per cent of the gross domestic product. This proportion has grown steadily throughout the twentieth century, save in times of war, and reached 16 per cent in 1975. Since then there has been a marked fall which has taken place under the guidance of both Conservative and Labour governments. Even so local authorities are still dealing with huge sums of money. The spending and collection of these funds necessarily raise many intricate problems.

A dominant feature of local finance is the meticulous care taken to control spending. Every authority prepares annually a detailed set of estimates to govern expenditure in the financial year starting on 1 April. Once approved by the council these estimates act as a check on subsequent expenditure. 'We cannot do anything about it this year because no provision has been made in the estimates' is a common explanation for failure to take action. If the political majority on an authority changes after an election there may be important and immediate changes of policy: if these involve extra expenditure, the initial budget must be altered with the possibility that an extra supplementary rate has to be levied. Such events are exceptional. Strict budgetary control is reinforced by auditing, by both internal and external auditors. Complicated rule systems have evolved to determine the legitimacy of expenditure. All this helps to prevent waste and corruption, although the auditing controls themselves cost a great deal of money.

The fact that local spending is subject to vigilant scrutiny does not stop this expenditure rising. Local authorities are affected by inflation like everyone else. A high proportion of the cost is labour cost; as wages and salaries go up, so must the outgoings. In money terms, spending can increase even when standards of service are falling. That is the present situation.

In local finance a careful distinction is made between revenue expenditure and capital expenditure. Capital spending involves the purchase of an asset which will last for years to come. Thus money spent on school-building or house-building is of a capital nature while the money spent on an official's salary is not. The distinction is important because local authorities can borrow to defray the cost of capital items. Not all capital spending is financed by borrowing; many small items are charged against current income. Loans have to be repaid and the cost of loan repayment including interest charges is included in revenue expenditure; such costs constitute a high proportion of revenue expenditure on housing.

Rather less than 60 per cent of current expenditure is now financed from central government grants. This overall figure conceals local variations because less prosperous areas enjoy levels of grant larger than the national average. The local rates withstand the highest proportion of expenditure in places where rateable values are high. Trading profits now make a negligible contribution to local resources. The Exchequer grants can be divided between the block grant which is a general subsidy to local government and a number of grants in support of specific services, for example, police and transport. The block grant is by far the more important factor amounting to nearly 90 per cent of the total national aid. On the expenditure side, the most costly service is education which accounts for roughly half of all the outgoings. For this reason one of the most common remedies suggested to ease the burden of the rates is to transfer the cost of teachers' salaries to central government.

While the global sums involved in local finance are immense, the financial resources of individual councils vary greatly, although the largest disparities were eliminated by the 1972 reorganisation. Figures for the rateable values of major authorities will be found in Appendix A. It has been assumed in the past, rather too easily, that low rateable value damages the quality of local services. In fact, quality probably depends more on the opinions of councillors than on the details of the local financial situation. Some of the poorest authorities, judged by the standard of rateable value per head, have maintained an excellent standard; partly this has been due to the central grant system and partly to decisions by councillors to incur expenditure that would involve a high rate poundage in the belief that their electors would accept that the money spent was well spent.

Every local council has to bear full responsibility for its own expenditure – subject to assistance from the central government. However, some expenditure is 'pooled'. This applies in the case of a specialised service which would be uneconomic for each authority to organise. So the service is provided by a particular council or some other agency in return for payment by other local authorities. Such arrangements cover advanced further education, approved schools, the training of teachers and 'no area' pupils, that is, pupils who are not the responsibility of any particular local education authority. Various formulae determine the details of these pooling schemes. One difficulty is that the authority providing the service may have little incentive to economise since it may itself have to defray but a small part of total expenditure. The problem has now been recognised, in particular by the Department of Education and Science, and cost limits have been placed on pooled education expenditure.

The great political problem of local finance is the level of the rate. Over the years agonised cries from ratepayers have persuaded the government to increase the level of central grants, to give special relief to domestic ratepayers, provide rebates for those with low incomes and, under the Conservative government, to encourage or require local authorities to increase rents and other charges. The cumulative result of these changes is quite dramatic, although not widely understood. In 1966, before the domestic rate relief and rate rebate arrangements started, the domestic ratepayer provided 19 per cent of the money spent by local authorities. This percentage had been falling slowly but the movement was gradual: ten years earlier the figure was 22 per cent. Now it has slumped to 8 per cent. The domestic ratepayer no longer make a significant contribution to local revenue. Non-domestic ratepayers have, in the past, been relatively quiet; now in a period of falling profits, they too are starting to complain.

The conclusion is inescapable. Political pressure against rate increases is so strong that the rate cannot provide an adequate, independent source of local revenue. The implications of this statement are examined in the final section of this chapter.

RATING

It was noted in Chapter 1 that the Elizabethan poor law laid the foundation for the present rating system. As local services developed their cost was met by extra rates added on to the parish poor rate: thus county rates and school board rates were linked with the poor rate. Such charges were imposed on the whole country, both town and rural areas. Urban areas had further expenses, mainly connected with sanitary services under the Public Health Acts, which were financed by a separate rate collected in boroughs and urban districts. In these areas two separate rates were imposed. Many towns obtained powers to unify the collection of money, but this wasteful and stupid duplication was not finally ended until 1925. Under the 1972 reorganisation the districts and the London boroughs levy the rate. Other authorities, the counties, the parishes and an assortment of joint boards with special powers, obtain income by precepting on the rating authorities. The level of the rate necessarily varies with local financial circumstances. Outside London it may vary within the area of a rating authority: in particular, wherever parish expenditure has to be added to the sums required to meet district and county expenses. In the non-metropolitan counties a very high proportion of rate revenue is handed on to the county councils because they are responsible for the most expensive services, notably education.

Liability to pay rates falls normally on the occupier of premises. Occupation is generally thought of in terms of control of the front door: a lodger does not control the front door and so is not liable. In some cases the owner of a property may be liable instead of the occupier(s). This applies to properties with a very low rateable value and to blocks of flats. Alternatively, an owner may come to an agreement with the rating authority to collect the rates from tenants along with the rents. For this trouble he receives a compounding allowance or discount from the rating authority. Until 1966 occupation was defined as beneficial occupation: no rates were payable on empty premises. However, rating authorities now have the option of imposing rates on premises unoccupied for three months, or six months in the case of new houses and flats. The Local Government Act 1974 also gave power to impose a penal rating surcharge on unoccupied office property. Some property is excused from payment. Agricultural land has been exempt since 1929. Crown land is also exempt; in practice, the Treasury makes an equivalent contribution. Property used for or in connection with religious worship, public parks, sewers, lighthouses, buoys, beacons, sheds for housing invalid chairs, and the residences of ambassadors and their servants, are also exempt; and so are certain classes of machinery not deemed to be part of a building. Almshouses and other properties used for charitable purposes enjoy a 50 per cent reduction in the amount of rates payable, and rating authorities have a discretionary power to remit their rates altogether. This discretionary power to reduce or remit rates extends to other non-profit-making institutions, for example, social clubs and educational, literary and scientific bodies.

How much is a ratepayer required to pay? This depends on two factors – the valuation placed on his property (the technical term is hereditament) and the poundage levied by the local rating authority. To give a simple example: if a house has a net assessment of £400 and the poundage charged is 125p, the liability for the year will be £500. It follows that valuation of properties for rating purposes is a matter of financial concern to every ratepayer. The valuation is an attempt to define the annual value of a hereditament. While all rating valuation is based on this single principle, various means are used to arrive at the assessment in relation to different classes of property. However, shops and houses are assessed on the basis of a reasonable rent for the property; this figure is known as the Gross Annual Value. There is a standard scale of allowances to cover maintenance and insurance costs which are deducted from the Gross Value and this produces a second and lower figure, the Net Annual Value, on which rates are actually paid. Other techniques of assessment are used for factories, licensed premises and nationalised industries.

The task of valuation has been carried out by the Inland Revenue since 1948. Originally, of course, it was the duty of the overseer. The Rating and Valuation Act 1925 abolished overseers and transferred the valuation function to county boroughs and area valuation committees which covered a group of neighbouring county districts. Finally the system was nationalised in 1948 to achieve uniformity. As a new system of government grants was introduced at this time designed to give greatest aid to authorities with the lowest rateable values per head of population, this uniformity was essential to ensure fairness in the distribution of the grant. In these circumstances the inducement to undervalue property would have been very strong. The first valuation list produced on a national basis became effective in 1956. In theory, a completely new valuation list is produced every five years, but they tend to be postponed. The 1961 revaluation was put off until 1963; the 1968 valuation was put back to 1973. No fresh valuation list has appeared since 1973 and it seems that there is no intention at present to produce another one. So valuation for rating fails to reflect the inflation of property prices. The whole system borders on a farce in that there is no relation between the law and the reality.

Any ratepayer may appeal against an assessment and argue his case before a local valuation court. A further appeal from a decision of this body can be made to the Lands Tribunal. To succeed an appeal must show that there is some injustice in the valuation. It is useless to go before the valuation court and say that you cannot afford to pay so much in rates. But if it can be shown that similar properties have a lower assessment, or that more desirable properties have the same assessment, or that the value of a property has been adversely affected by some local development, then an appeal can succeed.

In 1929 when agricultural land was derated altogether, industrial and freight-transport hereditaments were also relieved of three-quarters of their rate liability. But since the war the law on valuation for rating has been changed frequently in response to political and administrative pressures. In the 1963 valuation list the derating of industrial and freight-transport hereditaments was ended (Rating and Valuation Act 1961). Dwelling-houses, shops and offices are now rated also on current values, so there have been drastic upward adjustments everywhere in the assessments of residential property. Of course, the rate paid by the residential occupier does not increase *pro rata* with a rise in assessments because the rise in total rateable values, including the greater amounts accruing from industrial premises, should permit broadly equivalent reductions in the level of the rate poundage. But any ratepayer will suffer if his own assessment has risen proportionately more than the average assessments in his area. The rate burden also tends steadily to increase as local authorities are forced to pass on the rising charges for goods and services which they require.

The rating of nationalised industries presents a special problem; their physical assets are not Crown property but are assessable to rates. Three of them, the railways, the gas industry and the electricity supply industry, have fixed plant obviously not self-contained in any rating areas. Special arrangements operate under the General Rate Act 1967 for the ascertainment of the total rateable value of such assets in the areas of the owning Boards and the apportionment of the rate liabilities in respect of them among the rating authorities.

We now turn from valuation to the calculation of the rate poundage. The local financial year starts on 1 April, so in January and February estimates are prepared of spending in the coming financial year; these will be considered by a finance or central policy committee, possibly pruned back, and presented to the council for final approval. The detailed work is carried on by the Treasurer and his staff in consultation with the other spending committees. Obviously this involves pre-planning of future activities and requires important policy decisions to be made, so the preparation of estimates can be both a complex and controversial exercise. The final total of projected expenditure is a major feature of the local budget, but there are other factors which affect the extent of the demands made on ratepayers – national grants, local revenue from rents, fees and other charges and unspent balances, if any, from the previous year. A local authority is not entitled to accumulated surpluses on revenue account, so if expenditure in any one year is less than estimated, the saving should be devoted to reducing the rate levy in the following year. Of course, an adequate working balance is permitted and a margin for unexpected contingencies.

When the figures for the various parts of the budget are available, the size of the gap between expenditure and non-rate revenue becomes apparent. This is the gap that has to be filled by local taxation. If the charge on the rate fund shows a steep rise on the previous year, there may well be demands for reductions in expenditure. The rate poundage is fixed by relating the income required from the rate to the rateable value of a local authority's domain; the latter is the sum of the net rateable values of all properties in the area. Thus if a council has a rateable value of £5,000,000 and needs to raise £6,250,000, the probable levy is 126p in the £ – the extra penny being required to cover contingencies and the loss of revenue on empty property, various remissions and bad debts. This is, naturally, a greatly simplified picture of the local budgetary process; in reality, the calculations involved are highly complex. One other concept must be noticed, that of the penny rate product which is the amount produced by imposing a rate of a penny in the pound and equals one-hundredth of the local rateable value, ignoring the effect of empty property. The penny rate product is a useful way of showing the cost of any new policy. To revert to the earlier example, an authority with a rateable value of £5,000,000 has a penny rate worth £50,000, so that a £100,000 scheme that earned no revenue of its own and attracted no national grant would cost a twopenny rate.

In the 1960s the Labour government made two changes to reduce the burden on householders. The Rating Act 1966 was designed to ease the situation of ratepayers with low incomes. It authorised collection by instalments and provided for remission of rates for poorer persons not in receipt of national assistance. Each applicant for a rebate has to submit to a means test; the amount of relief granted depends upon a scale which is adjusted from time to time, to take account of changes in the value of money. Ninety per cent of the cost of these concessions is met by a government grant. In fact, fewer people have applied for rebates than was initially anticipated. All domestic ratepayers, rich and poor alike, benefit from a lower poundage levied on their properties. The initial reduction in 1967 was 2·1p and a government subsidy made good the financial loss to local government. Now the reduction is 18·5p and the cost of this arrangement is covered in the annual block grant paid to local authorities.

GOVERNMENT GRANTS

When the state required local government to undertake new duties it often made a grant in aid of the new service to ease the financial burden. Alternatively, grants were given to reduce the cost of an activity obviously of national as well as local benefit; a clear example is the grant made to meet the cost of criminal prosecutions in 1834. There is, of course, room for argument over which services are of national benefit. Public health is of national interest because disease can spread across local authority boundaries. An efficient police force is of national benefit whereas a local playing field is not. Through the years views have changed on the nature and extent of the public interest and the term is now given a much wider definition than in the nineteenth century. The Victorian controversy about the exact distinction between what were described as local beneficial services and national onerous services deserving national aid now seems curiously antique. However, this distinction had an important role in the evolution of the grant system. Grants were also given to ease the burdens of the poorer areas and to ensure that minimum standards were maintained over services thought to be of national importance. Financial recompense also has had to be made to local councils when the national government reduces their taxing powers, for example, the derating of agricultural land and the partial derating of industry in 1929 and the domestic rate relief imposed by the Local Government Act 1966.

There has been a succession of changes in government financial policy towards local authorities. Various types of grant have been used. The main distinction is between specific grants and general grants. The specific grant is given to aid a particular local service and is usually given on a percentage basis. An alternative is a unit basis – so much per house or flat. The percentage arrangement has two disadvantages. It may encourage extravagant spending, especially if the percentage grant is high: where a 50 per cent grant applies, the local authority can expect to recover half its expenditure. In consequence, central departments have to impose some check on local expenditure, probably by setting down categories of spending that will be accepted for grant purposes. This involves more central supervision of local government and an increase in administrative cost.

The major specific grants now relate to police and transport. For the police the government provides 50 per cent of local expenditure subject to being satisfied about the efficiency of the local force. While many other specific grants have disappeared, the police grant remains because the Home Office believes that the grant is a useful means of supporting central supervision. The transport supplementary grant (TSG) was introduced in 1974; the amount is determined in the annual discussions on the size of the general grant – now termed the block grant. The TSG relates to local expenditure on highways, public transport subsidies and traffic regulation. To explain and justify their spending programmes each county council has to submit to central government a document entitled Transport Policy and Programme (TPP) which contains a statement of transport objectives and strategy over the next decade or so. The TSG/TPP system is a clear example of the strong link between specific grants and central control; in 1977 the transport grant for South Yorkshire was cut drastically because the government opposed the local policy of providing large subsidies to keep down the level of bus fares.

The Local Government Act 1974 also provided that central government would meet 90 per cent of the cost of awards to students at universities and teacher training colleges or following courses of equivalent standard. The Layfield Report was notably unenthusiastic about specific grants. It urged that the whole cost of mandatory awards be met by the government; because local authorities had no discretion, they should not be required to pay. The report also proposed that the police and transport subsidies should be merged into the general grant system.

A general grant is a contribution to local rate funds not linked to any particular function or purpose. It can be designed to help only the poorer authorities or it can be given to all. The present block grant combines both these features. A general grant is simpler administratively. Arguably it is more conducive to local independence and freedom from central supervision. It also encourages good housekeeping by local authorities. The amount of grant is fixed before the start of a financial year so the councils know in advance their income from the government. Any extra sums they may be tempted to spend fall squarely on the rates. Quite naturally, the general grants method has always been preferred by the Treasury. Essentially the history of the grant system over the past hundred years is one of continuous growth but also of ebb and flow between the general and specific categories. In 1888, 1929 and again in 1958 many specific grants were swept away and replaced by (more) general grants.

Government financial aid to local authorities is now dominated by the block grant introduced by the Local Government, Planning and Land Act 1980. It covers over 90 per cent of central aid to local authorities and incorporates the cost of the rate poundage relief given to all domestic ratepayers. Complex annual discussions are held over the size of the block grant. Representatives of central and local government, the latter nominated through the associations of local authorities, examine estimates of future expenditure in great detail. Since 1975 these talks have been held under the aegis of the

Consultative Council for Local Government Finance. Inevitably the government holds the whip hand in these negotiations both because it is providing the money and because local expenditure is now so large that it is made to conform with the economic policy of the Cabinet. The Labour and Conservative Parties may have differing views of how the country should be run, but both agree that local government must be made to fit in with their own pattern of priorities. In the 1980s the relations between central and local government are strained because of Conservative insistence on lower public spending, but reductions in the central grant and cuts in local activities go back to 1976 when Labour was in office.

An important difference between the block grant and its predecessor, the rate support grant (RSG), is that the amount now obtained by a local council does not bear a fixed relationship to its expenditure: under the replaced RSG formula, the sums distributed were influenced by local rate poundages, so that if a local authority imposed a high rate, it also got more from the government. For Conservatives, keen to reduce public spending, such an arrangement was intolerable. Vice was being subsidised and therefore encouraged.

The basis of the allocation of the block grant involves obstruse statistical calculations, understood only by a limited group of specialists. A calculation is made of what it would cost each county and district to provide the range and standard of service that central government considers reasonable. Such an assessment must take account of the functions of an authority, its population and the character and prosperity of the area. An estimate is made of future price levels – an allowance for inflation – which is normally inadequate. At the end of the process for each county and district there emerges a GREA, grant related expenditure assessment. The total grant distributed by the government is 56 per cent of the sum of the GREAs. The sum received by each council will depend on local circumstances and its own decisions about spending. The higher the level of local spending per head of population, the lower is the rate of grant. Once local expenditure goes beyond 110 per cent of grant related expenditure per head then the ratio of grant aid falls away sharply. Thus the block grant system offers strong inducements towards economy. As councils spend more, the ratepayers bear a higher share of the cost.

For every local authority the amount of its own GREA could be a source of discontent. Critics have suggested that the GREAs favoured the shire counties at the expense of the metropolitan authorities. Since metropolitan councils are mostly Labour controlled there is a possibility of political discrimination. Yet the main

controversy surrounding this system is not about these assessments: the trouble arises over the power of the Secretaries of State
for the Environment and for Wales to reduce or withhold grant as
a penalty if they consider local spending is too high. Policies for
England and Wales need not be the same. The targets for expenditure which the Conservative government imposed on local authorities are related not to the GREAs but to the level of spending in
each local authority in 1978–9. Thus local authorities are presented with two yardsticks to restrain expenditure, one relating to
their own past behaviour and the other being the government's
present view of what is appropriate in the particular local circumstances. Those authorities whose spending exceeds the higher of
these alternatives suffer a penalty with a 'holdback' of part of the
grant they otherwise would have received. Where an authority
has passed out of Conservative control in recent elections, the
new group majority will favour higher spending but, if it puts its
policy into practice, the result will be a severe financial penalty.
The grant system can be regarded as a means to thwart the
consequences of local elections.

This is not the place to discuss the merits of the economic policy of
any particular government. But how far would marginal increases in
local expenditure in some areas, paid for through the rates, really
damage the whole of a national economic strategy? Local
authorities may also feel aggrieved that central government is
asking them to do what central government cannot do to itself.
Whitehall spends more whichever party is in power. In 1975 local
government was responsible for 35 per cent of government expenditure; by 1980 this figure had fallen to 29 per cent. This movement is
partly due to local cutbacks but the major influence is the increases
in central spending mostly on defence, unemployment pay and
social welfare benefits. Viewed against this background the central
insistence on local parsimony seems even more unreasonable.

CAPITAL EXPENDITURE

Local authorities may borrow money to meet the cost of capital
expenditure, subject to the consent of the Department of the
Environment. Each loan has to be paid back over a period of years,
the length of the period depending on the durability of the asset. The
lifespan of capital assets is estimated on a conservative basis for this
purpose; for example, loans for baths and wash-houses must be
repaid over thirty years, for houses over sixty years, for housing land
over eighty years. It follows that at the end of these periods the local
authority will have a debt-free asset; it may achieve this position

even earlier for no council is compelled to borrow for the maximum permissible period.

Inevitably this raises the question, is it a good policy to borrow at all? An individual with an adequate income but no capital who seeks to buy a house has no alternative: he must try to borrow by raising a mortgage. But a local authority is not in the same situation. It has a flexible source of revenue and can increase its income by raising the rate poundage. Should ratepayers be forced to pay for capital assets immediately, without recourse to borrowing? This policy has one great advantage – cheapness. To raise a loan for a period as long as sixty years is extremely expensive. Interest rates are now very high. At the time of writing local authorities are having to pay 13 per cent. (Of course, if the rate of interest is below the rate of inflation, the lender stands to lose – quite apart from the tax that has to be paid on the interest received.) So local authorities can save money by paying for capital assets out of revenue, and a few councils did so in relation to at least part of their capital expenditure until the last war. Now the policy is out of favour for a variety of reasons. Durable assets will be of benefit to the next generation of ratepayers, so why should the whole cost be met by the ratepayers of today? This is a powerful argument which is reinforced by the continuous tendency for the purchasing power of the pound to decline. A pound borrowed now will buy much more than it will when repaid in, say, fifty years time; admittedly this is only a prediction but all economic experience suggests it is a safe one! The faster the depreciation of currency, the greater the advantage to the debtor, the greater the loss to the creditor. The advantage to the debtor is offset by the interest that has to be paid but, unless interest rates are high, there is potential advantage in borrowing. At present interest rates are high, very high, and this encourages many authorities to charge small capital items to current revenue. To charge large capital sums to the rate fund would involve raising rate levels even more steeply and this would be politically unacceptable. If major capital schemes were financed from revenue, there is a danger that standards of provision would become not merely economical but parsimonious.

Ministerial control over local borrowing was firmly established by the end of the nineteenth century. The reasons for control of borrowing have changed over the years. Originally, the concern was to ensure that local authorities were not overstepping the limits of their financial resources by incurring unduly heavy commitments for the future repayment of debt. Such Gladstonian prudence has now gone. The central government was also concerned to ensure that engineering proposals by local authorities were technically sound:

smaller authorities with inadequate specialist advice had to be protected from the possibility of expensive mistakes. Now the main task is to ensure that capital spending by local authorities is in conformity with the government's overall economic programme and, indeed, is in conformity with ministers' patterns of priorities.

Capital construction schemes are allocated priorities two or three years in advance. To save administrative work loan sanction may be given not for individual projects but for a whole programme of construction. Once ministerial permission to borrow has been obtained, a local authority – and its Treasurer – are faced with two interrelated problems, how to obtain the loan and whether it is preferable to borrow on a short-term or long-term basis. The latter question involves attempting to forecast the future pattern of interest rates. If they are expected to rise, it is better to arrange a long-term loan with a fixed interest: if a fall is anticipated, it is better to arrange a short period loan so that the money can be reborrowed subsequently at a lower interest charge. From time to time the Treasury has expressed concern over the pattern of local authority debt. It has been worried that loan periods are too short. Local financial officers, hoping that interest rates will fall, have tended to opt for short-term borrowing. However, this policy creates a need for incessant re-borrowing, increases the instability of the capital market, creates a greater likelihood of default and magnifies the impact of changes in interest rates on local finances. A voluntary code of practice has been agreed between local authorities and the government which will have the effect of steadily lengthening the average period of loans. Central supervision over local borrowing has also been strengthened to control the amount of capital expenditure within a given financial year. Previously the loan sanction arrangements had been related to projects or programmes and did not determine dates within which the sanction could be used. Thus the capital schemes of local councils are forced to fit in with the government's annual plans for public expenditure and become a buttress of national economic policy.

Various techniques of raising capital are available to a local authority. One is the Public Works Loan Board, established under an Act of 1875. The Board is financed by government loans and the Treasury prescribes the interest rates to be charged. In recent years there have been a number of shifts of government policy in relation to the PWLB. Originally the idea was that the Board should assist mainly the smaller authorities which lacked both the prestige and experience to raise funds easily in the money market. The tendency is still for the smaller authorities and those in less prosperous areas to make greatest use of the PWLB.

Other techniques of borrowing can be described briefly. Subject to Treasury consent, local authorities can issue stock. Relatively large sums of money can be obtained by this means for a long period and these advantages are important to large authorities when interest rates are not too high. The most common methods are to issue mortgages or bonds. For technical reasons the bonds are simpler to administer and so are coming more into favour. Some capital is available from internal sources, for example, superannuation funds. Short-period and temporary loans are raised through the money market or from banks.

A general picture of local authority indebtedness can be obtained from the figures published by the Chartered Institute of Public Finance and Accountancy which show how capital debt has been utilised and the source of borrowing.

ANALYSIS OF LOCAL AUTHORITY DEBT, 1980

by service	£000,000	by form of debt	%
Housing:		Stock	4·4
Housing Revenue a/c	21,701	Bonds and mortgages	30·1
Other	4,145	PWLB	36·1
Education	4,410	Temporary loans	14·7
Highways	1,675	Internal advances	2·3
Environmental Services	1,056	Revenue	9·5
Planning and Development	897	Other	2·9
Trading Services	811		—
Leisure and Recreation	596		
Social Services	568		
Police and Fire	265		
Other	414		
Total	36·538		

Source: CIPFA: Summary of Debt Outstanding

For the general public and the councillors the amounts to be spent on capital account and the projects chosen are more significant than the technicalities of borrowing. Central government is also deeply concerned with the total of capital expenditure. The annual White Papers on Public Expenditure set out targets for local spending and local authorities have managed to keep close to these limits in spite of the fact that they have sometimes been revised downwards after initial publication. Yet the Thatcher government decided to strengthen further its supervision of capital expenditure undertaken by local councils.

The new system was introduced under the Local Government, Planning and Land Act 1980 and operated as from April 1981. Capital expenditure is divided in five 'blocks' – Housing, Education, Social Services, Transport and Other. This arrangement covers all local activities except the police: here the expenditure is authorised separately by the Home Office. Each local authority has to submit each financial year a bid to the appropriate government department for permission to spend so much on capital items within the range covered by a block. Different categories of authorities produce different numbers of bids. A shire county has four covering Education, Social Services, Transport and Other while a shire district has two, Housing and Other. The bids include not only proposals for the coming financial year but should also look some way in the future.

Why did the government feel that this new system was needed? The previous method of giving approval to borrow for particular projects or programmes had not worked badly, at least in the sense that total expenditure targets had been met. The difficulty was that control of borrowing appeared to be getting weaker as a technique of control. In 1970 less than a quarter of capital expenditure was financed by means other than borrowing; ten years later borrowing covered no more than two-thirds of capital costs. The remainder was produced by rate revenue, leasing, sale of capital assets and the use of internal funds, for example, superannuation funds. So control through borrowing left a large loophole, and one that could be exploited further by local authorities politically opposed to the Conservative government. The solution was thus a blanket-control over capital expenditure. Even so, one loophole is left. Local authorities can still use funds obtained from the sale of assets as they choose; this tolerance is designed to encourage the sale of council property, especially council houses. On the other hand, it will not be possible to evade the new control by simply charging purchases to a current account: each item over £5,000 is to be regarded as a capital acquisition.

While the new system is all-embracing, it does contain elements of flexibility. Thus once a council has received permission to spend a certain sum, it can go ahead without further heed of central government. It can change its priorities within a 'block'. It can switch money between blocks – a process known as virement. If a local authority fails to spend the permitted sum then it can 'keep' 10 per cent to spend in the following year. Any further unspent balance can be passed on to a neighbouring local authority provided it is spent in the same year. There appears to be a philosophy behind this code of rules: that the government does not care how local authorities spend money, provided they keep within the global Treasury target for local capital expenditure.

How is the control over capital expenditure enforced? An authority that exceeds the permitted ceilings will not, at least initially, be acting unlawfully. But if the secretary of state is of opinion that the financial limits have been breached deliberately and substantially then he has power to require local authorities not to exceed the limits in future. Further, he may require that substantial contracts require special approval or direct an authority not to spend its capital authorisation on particular projects. Any disobedience to such instructions will constitute *ultra vires* actions. So the government has provided itself with reserve powers to ensure that its will prevails.

There remains the question whether the scheme will work as its authors intended. The idea that local authorities will have more freedom may be illusory. If a council decides to change its priorities and spend in a way that does not accord with Whitehall policy, what will be the fate of that council's bids in subsequent years? There is an old saying that 'He who pays the piper calls the tune'. In the present context the adage is not quite apt because the central government is not paying. The position, however, is that he who allows the piper to play calls the tune.

Another major problem is timing. Under the old method of authorising local borrowing, the speed at which capital works were completed did not affect government permission. Now that only so much must be spent on capital account each year, the speed of a major capital scheme becomes crucial. And it may also be extremely difficult to estimate in advance. The timetable at the start of an important scheme can be particularly awkward. Such a scheme must be included in a bid prepared early in the financial year before work was due to start. Preliminary design work must precede the bid. If the land required is not already in council ownership, its acquisition must be delayed until the bid has been successful. Yet any delays in obtaining the site, or in obtaining planning permission, could delay the construction schedule. On the other hand, if a scheme moved forward more easily than expected, progress in construction that was practicable and economically desirable could be delayed by the operation of the annual capital limits.

RATES – INADEQUATE AND UNFAIR?

Rates probably cause more irritation than any other form of taxation. Before examining the causes of this discontent, it is well to look at the few advantages that can be claimed for the rates. The rating mechanism, in spite of complexities of detail, is traditional and is well understood. Now assessment has been nationalised, the valuations are generally just and, in any case, can be challenged by appeals. Since rates are payable on visible and immovable property, it is impossible to avoid paying. This means that the local authorities have a stable and reliable source of revenue. Rates are also a flexible tax in that it is easy to alter the level of the poundage. They are also economical to collect: according to the County Councils Association the collection cost is 1·2 per cent of the total revenue. Since rates are a tax on housing they act as a deterrent to under-occupation of property and may encourage people with excess accommodation to sub-let or move. And as the rates are imposed by local authorities they provide a degree of financial independence from the central government; without such independence, local councils would soon become mere agents of central departments spending from national funds. This last item in the catalogue is not an argument for rates *per se*, but it is an argument of basic importance for the retention by local authorities of an independent taxing capacity. So far no alternative to the rates has appeared to be politically or administratively acceptable; in these circumstances, the rates remain a bulwark of local autonomy.

Why then do rates provoke criticism? The first answer is psychological. Rates are a very obvious tax. Indirect taxes, for example, those on tobacco, beer and petrol, are linked with the natural cost of the commodity: the public is generally aware that there is a substantial tax element in the total price, but the price is still accepted as the price *of the commodity*. Anyone entering a tobacconist's shop is not dominated by the thought that he is about to make a contribution to national revenue. Income tax, for the most part, is collected on a 'pay as you earn' basis, so the wage- and salary-earner comes to accept the net amount of his weekly or monthly pay-slip as his true income. The tax and insurance deductions are accepted, no doubt regretted, but ignored when it comes to planning personal expenditure. You do not miss what you have never had. In contrast to PAYE and indirect taxes, the rates are not hidden in any way. Since rates are usually payable on a half-yearly basis, the sum involved on each occasion is substantial: however, authorities are now less unwilling to collect by more frequent instalments. Yet it still remains true that taxpayers are more conscious of rates than of other forms of taxation. Other people may not share this awareness. And this is important because in 1945 when universal suffrage was extended to local government, a substantial gap developed between the number of people paying rates and those who can vote for councillors who impose rates.

Those who suffer financial responsibility no longer correspond with those who exercise constitutional power. But this distinction should not be overstressed. Local authorities now obtain more revenue from grants than they do from the local rate and everyone is liable to contribute to national taxes. Further, adult members of a household normally contribute to its expenses and rent for furnished accommodation should contain a rate element.

There are many other objections. From the point of view of the local authority, the rates have an unsatisfactory tax base. Prices and costs rise ceaselessly; property values also rise but the quinquennial valuations are always postponed so that rateable values do not keep pace with the fall in the purchasing power of money. This means that rate poundages are forced up almost every year, thus creating annual discontent. It is also arguable that the reasonable rent basis of valuation for domestic property is largely spurious because, owing to the operation of rent restriction legislation, in many areas there is no free market in rented property. More equitable assessments might be achieved if capital values were used instead of hypothetical rental values. Householders may be deterred from expanding or improving their properties since to do so involves a bigger rate liability. There is also no connection between the use a ratepayer makes of local services and the extent of his rate bill. Whether this is a valid objection is a matter of opinion. Personal demands upon local services are either a matter of choice or need and, in so far as they result from need, the rate-supported services contribute to social equality. It is certain that areas in which the need for social welfare provision is greatest have the lowest rateable values per head; *vice versa* where needs are less, rateable values are high. This creates a situation in which it is easiest to raise rate revenue where it is least required as high rateable values tend to produce low rate poundages. The system of government grants is designed to assist the poorer areas, but they do not entirely eliminate disparities.

All this makes up a powerful case against rates. A further criticism is that high rates increase unemployment. By forcing up costs in industry, commerce, tourism and the retail trade they increase prices beyond what the consumer is willing to pay. So demand falls and jobs are lost. Perhaps this argument is exaggerated since rates form only a small part of the costs of most business enterprises. It is also the case that those who are liable to pay in relation to shop, commercial and industrial premises can use their rate bill as an expense for which an allowance is made in relation to income tax liability. No such relief is available for the domestic ratepayer. Indeed, it is arguable that to give income tax relief for rate liability

would be unfair since it would give no aid to those who need it most –
those too poor to pay income tax.

In 1963 there was a great outcry about the unfairness of rating
after the new valuation list had reassessed residential properties at
current values. The storm of protest forced the government to
appoint a committee to inquire into the impact of local rates on
households. This committee, under the chairmanship of Professor
Allen, issued its report in 1965 and demonstrated clearly the
regressive nature of local rates. Their incidence is quite different to
income tax. A man with a large family enjoys substantial allowances
in respect of his children when income tax is computed. He also
needs to occupy more residential accommodation if he can afford it –
and this will make him liable to pay more rates. A lodger pays no
rates at all, at least directly. When the rating system was instituted
on a national scale in 1601 it was broadly fair as between individuals
since it was based on visible wealth, and the squire in the manor
house could obviously afford to pay more than the tenant farmer or
the yeoman. Today the size of a property is an unsure guide to the
wealth of its occupants and their ability to contribute to the cost of
local services.

However, the situation has altered dramatically since 1965. The
Layfield Report showed that in 1975 households with a weekly
income below £20 made no net contribution to the rates; above £20 a
week the rates had a slowly increasing impact until a plateau was
reached at income levels between £35 and £80 a week when the rates
claimed between 2 and 3 per cent of income; above £80 a week the
rate demand consumes a diminishing proportion of income. So the
regressive effect of local rates has been substantially diminished.
Three factors have contributed to the change. More generous
supplementary benefits have assisted low income groups to pay their
rates. The Rating Act 1966 provided for remission of rates for the
poorest sections of the community, subject to a means test. The
Local Government Act 1966 introduced a national subsidy to enable
lower rates to be charged on all residential properties. This benefit is
not subject to any income limitation and, as shown above, has been
increased substantially over the years. Thus a great deal has been
done to mitigate the hardships caused by the rating system but,
because public memory is short, the extent of the improvement
tends to be forgotten. Meanwhile, the policy of rate relief has one
serious drawback – local government tends to become more
financially dependent on the national Exchequer. And, inevitably
the influence of ministers becomes even stronger.

Widespread concern about the rating system led to the appointment of the Layfield Committee. Its report, *Local Government*

Finance (Cmnd 6453), published in 1976, provided a fundamental reassessment of the subject. However, its suggestions were mostly too radical to receive support from either of the major political parties. A main theme of the report was that local government would be greatly strengthened if it were given a stronger independent tax base. However, national politicians may not welcome the idea of stronger local government because many local authorities are always likely to have ideas about policy which conflict with those of ministers. As a result no action has been taken on the Layfield proposal that property be assessed on the basis of capital value rather than annual value. Another Layfield suggestion, to abolish agricultural derating, has been officially rejected. Such adjustments would strengthen the rating system but they do not really get to the heart of the problem. A satisfactory solution demands a new base for local taxation. Motor taxation duties might be transferred to local authorities. But if the *level* of charge were to be fixed locally, then it would be cheaper to register vehicles in some places than others: it might well become economic to garage large lorry fleets in areas with lower duties. Yet if the level of tax is not a matter for local decision, councils have no control over their incomes. A sales tax is more obviously capable of local adjustment, but it faces three major objections. Presumably it would be in addition to the national VAT and obviously would be a most unwelcome addition. Like the rates it would be regressive in that, unless restricted to luxury and semi-luxury goods, the burden would be heaviest on the poorest members of the community. Finally, people living in the countryside and in small towns spend money in bigger towns. To take the extreme case, London is almost a national shopping centre. So if the tax were collected by the present rating authorities on turnover in their own districts, rural areas would suffer badly. Were local government organised on a regional basis, this obstacle would partly disappear.

The idea of a local income tax has been widely canvassed for many years. It would add greatly to the financial independence of local government. As compared with a rate on property, it has the advantage that more people would be required to contribute to local revenues. The sums paid by individuals might also be more fairly related to their ability to pay; whether those with low incomes would benefit depends on the rules adopted for rate rebates and income tax relief. The Layfield Report suggested that local income tax should supplement local rates. It should be levied by local authorities that face the highest expenditure, the shire counties, the metropolitan districts and the London boroughs. However, the Layfield Report listed many practical difficulties to be faced. Expense is a serious obstacle. Rather than establish new local income tax offices, it would be cheaper to use the services of the Inland Revenue: however, the methods of the Revenue would need adjustment since income tax collection is based on the location of employers not on the residence of employees. Another problem is that at present national taxes are uniform; local income tax requires collection at varied levels. By the use of the Inland Revenue, Layfield estimated that administrative costs could be kept down to £100 million per annum at 1975 prices. As the work of the Inland Revenue becomes computerised, one would have thought that this cost could be substantially reduced.

Not surprisingly the government's Green Paper issued in response to the Layfield Report (Cmnd 6813) rejected local income tax. The Treasury could be expected to resist any interference by local government with a key regulator of the economy. The Green Paper commented that local freedom 'to vary the LIT rate would have to be closely constrained so that it did not unduly complicate central government economic and financial management'. And if LIT were absorbed in PAYE deductions, the public would tend to lose sight of it; local accountability, so heavily emphasised by Layfield, would be lost.

It must be stressed that the Layfield support for local income tax was hedged by the stipulation that it should be linked with 'express moves towards giving greater power of decision to local authorities'. So the proposed reform was specifically associated with the wider question of relations between central and local government.

Until 1975 local government services expanded at a faster rate than the growth of the national economy. It followed that rate revenue had to increase not merely in monetary terms but as a proportion of the national product unless one of four other possibilities was adopted. These were a reduction in the scale of growth of local services; higher levels of central government grants; removal of some services from the ambit of local government; the development of other sources of revenue for local authorities. The first alternative slows down progress; the second implies loss of independence; the third weakens local government by limiting its scope. Clearly the fourth solution is the most acceptable to local authorities. In practice, the second and third alternatives were followed.

The arrival of the Thatcher government produced a marked change of emphasis: the first and fourth alternatives have come to the fore. No longer is there a prospect of expanding local services. The argument has changed to one about cuts, how big they should be and where should they fall. Since the cuts adversely affect local authority staff and those who appreciate the benefits derived from local services, the arguments are vigorous. The fourth alternative to higher rates, other sources of local revenue, has also been pursued but in the context of more charges for local services rather than schemes for new forms of taxation. Conservative philosophy seeks a reduction in public expenditure achieved partly by withholding benefits from those who can afford to do without them. Accordingly the government expects local authorities to increase the charges for school meals so as to cover their full cost. Legislation in 1980 authorised the imposition of fees in relation to planning applications. Other charges, notably council house rents, are steadily increased. Restrictions on transport grants have an impact on bus services. Another means of increasing local revenue is to sell assets: the Conservatives favour the sale of council houses. Leaving aside the social consequences of this policy, it is a matter for argument whether the sale of capital assets at discount prices really helps the financial state of local councils. But the Conservatives yearn for a fuller acceptance of a private enterprise, free-market economy and, perforce, the financial affairs of local authorities are manipulated towards achieving this aim.

There remains the question of the future of the rating system. Both the Conservative and Labour Parties would like to get rid of it but they are not clear what to put in its place. The Conservative election manifesto in October 1974 states 'we shall abolish the domestic rating system and replace it by taxes more broadly based and related to people's ability to pay'. By 1979 the party was more cautious and merely noted that 'cutting income tax must take priority for the time being over abolition of the domestic rating system'. So there is a policy vacuum. It is significant that revaluation of property for rating purposes has been abandoned. Any future reassessment related to current prices would produce dramatic results. Most assessments would have to be multiplied by between ten and twenty times. Rating valuations are now often below 1 per cent of the capital value of property. The foundation of local taxation – rateable value – has been allowed to decay. Any attempt to restore it would provoke a political outcry that no government would be eager to face.

The government's attempts to limit local spending have added fuel to the controversy about rates. In the autumn of 1981 a Local Government Bill was introduced which would have restricted the level of the rate a local authority could impose. If this amount was felt to be insufficient a further, limited supplementary rate could be levied. If an authority wanted yet more revenue it had to hold a local referendum to give it power to impose a second supplementary rate. This scheme involved a fresh and major restriction on the rights of local councillors which called into question the whole concept of local representative democracy. After widespread protests, not least from Conservative circles, the legislation was withdrawn. Subsequently an Act was passed which banned supplementary rates altogether but imposed no limit on the normal annual rate levy. The prospect is that councils may feel forced to charge slightly higher rates than would otherwise be required in order to maintain a reserve against contingencies.

In December 1981 a Green Paper was issued, *Alternatives to Domestic Rates* (Cmnd 8449). The document reviewed the possibilities of the complete or partial replacement of the rating system. To a large extent it retraced the ground covered by the Layfield Committee. The one fresh idea was a poll tax; anyone on the electors register would have to pay a flat rate tax. However, it was recognised that there would also be difficulties in preventing evasion. Such a tax would also be highly regressive. It would bear most heavily upon those with the lowest incomes and, even if some people were excused from payment, the regressive tendency would still apply to all those who did pay. The Green Paper repeated the problems surrounding local income tax and sales tax which were discussed above. Certainly, it has no clear message. A Green Paper is intended to be a discussion document; it is difficult to see that further discussion will lead to a satisfactory form of local taxation.

Chapter 6

CENTRAL CONTROL

Relations between local authorities and the central government are rarely static and always uneasy. The nature of national concern with local administration changes over time. In the nineteenth century the major issue was the poor law. Not only was it the most expensive local service but it had a profound effect on the lives of many members of the community: it offered opportunities for corruption and incompetence: central government could not ignore the activities of the local Guardians. But there was little positive enthusiasm at the centre for interference in local affairs. Such intervention was regarded as an unfortunate necessity, but sometimes needed to ensure that local business was properly conducted.

Today, the atmosphere has wholly changed. The centre believes it to be right and proper that national decisions should guide and shape local decisions. Local government has come to accept more central supervision, even if complaints are frequent about particular controls or threats of imposition of yet further restrictions. Clearly, if the national government did not have ultimate control over local councils the latter would tend to become autonomous units. No sovereign state would tolerate such a basic challenge to its authority unless it was prepared to become a federation of largely independent communities. At the other extreme, if local government were to have no ambit of decision not dominated by national government – then it would cease to be local *government* at all and become a mere agent of national government. So central–local relations demand a balance of control and independence, a balance of partnership and separation. The vital question now is whether the element of control has become so strong as to undermine the concept of local government.

The orthodox treatment of central control divides it into three categories: supervision by Parliament, by government departments and by the courts. This fits the traditional tripartite division of political institutions into the legislature, the executive and the judiciary. However, if this model induces the idea that local government has three sets of controllers – Members of Parliament, civil servants and judges – then it is misleading. Civil servants advise ministers how to use the powers made available to them by Act of Parliament. Members of Parliament are heavily influenced by party loyalty, so that the Commons normally accept the policy proposed by ministers of the government. Not all legislation is initiated by ministers and the formal process of party discipline, the use of the whips, is not applied to Bills sponsored by backbenchers or by local authorities. But no Bill in either of these categories will pass if ministers are deeply hostile to it. Thus both parliamentary and administrative controls over local government reflect the will of ministers. Judicial control is a separate category; yet here again if ministers dislike a judicial interpretation of local government law they could use their parliamentary majority to amend the law.

The legal basis of national control over local government is that local authorities have no powers other than those conferred on them by statute. All local councils must be able to produce statutory authority for everything they do. If a council exceeds its powers, albeit unwittingly, its actions may be challenged in court where the principle of *ultra vires* will be invoked, and the extra-legal actions will be declared null and void. Thus local authorities largely carry out the administration of general principles of policy decided by the national legislature. Local authorities are not themselves legislative – that is, rule-making – bodies except in relation to local by-laws, and even here their decisions are subject to detailed government scrutiny and approval.

Local government law is complex, partly because it contains so much detail, partly because there are different categories of enabling legislation. The basic constitutional rules are set out in the Local Government Act 1972. Powers relating to a particular function are commonly to be found in legislation limited to that specific topic; obvious examples are the major Acts dealing with public health, education and town and country planning. Even so, the Local Government Act 1972 contains many provisions relating to particular duties. Local government law also incorporates many provisions which enable ministers and their civil servants to influence local events – a topic examined in the following section of this chapter. Further complications are added because the law is always changing, so that parts of older laws are still operative while other sections have been replaced and repealed. And, as noted in Chapter 3, a local authority may seek to gain extra powers by a local Act. So the law of local government is not entirely uniform and on matters of minor detail may vary from place to place. In addition to powers obtained directly from statutes, local government receives further powers from various types of Orders made by ministers – Provisional Orders, Orders under the Statutory Orders (Special Procedure) Act 1945 and normal Statutory Instruments. These are subject to varying degrees of parliamentary scrutiny. However, since they all engage the influence of ministers, it is unusual for any parliamentary challenge to be successful. Many Orders of purely local application, for example, compulsory purchase and clearance orders, asked for by local authorities, are approved or not approved by ministers, and are not submitted to Parliament at all.

There can be little doubt that this tight legal corset has had a profound effect on the outlook of those engaged in local administration. Officials are conditioned to keep a constant eye on legal minutae. Other public servants are also governed by statutory provisions but few are so deeply conscious of legal limitations as are local authority administrators. Similarly, councillors have to live with a permanent threat of personal financial penalty if they use their powers in a manner subsequently judged to be illegal. Ministers and Members of Parliament are not treated in this way. Nor are those who sit on the wide variety of public boards now commonly described as quangoes. Since the nineteenth century councillors have been keen for legal advice to be readily available so that they do not unwittingly transgress the law and suffer thereby. For this reason local authorities, big enough and rich enough to be able to afford it, liked to appoint a lawyer to be clerk of the authority. The very natural concern of councillors for self-protection has thus ensured that the legal profession has built up a powerful role in local government. A legal voice tends to inhibit. It advises that risk should be avoided, that all eventualities be covered. Whether too much weight is sometimes given to professional advice can be a matter for discussion. Elected representatives may allow their wishes to be over-borne by the arguments presented by officials with specialised qualifications. Advice from a solicitor can scarcely fail to be highly influential. The complexity of the law reinforces the need for such counsel and perforce must have a dampening effect on local affairs.

Parliament has been cautious in granting powers to local authorities in order to restrict their ability to interfere with private citizens, especially in relation to property rights. The Victorians were determined to keep the power of the state firmly in check. If Parliament granted powers to local bodies, it was even more important that such powers were strictly curtailed. There may now be a rather more cavalier attitude amongst central departments towards individual rights but for local administration much of the Victorian legacy remains, reinforced by a fresh ministerial desire to limit scope for variations in the local services provided.

This web of law is enforced and interpreted by the courts. Litigation has had an important influence on the development of local government. Until the latter half of the nineteenth century Whitehall departments had limited personnel and resources; administrative supervision of local government in the modern style was impossible before a substantial civil service had been established. County justices exercised somewhat erratic supervision over parish officers but the justices themselves and the municipal corporations enjoyed considerable independence. The means of redress for a citizen disgruntled with a local authority was to bring a legal action, but such action was likely to be started only by the wealthy. So judicial control was spasmodic. But certain legal principles inherited from the past, notably *ultra vires*, are of major significance.

The general effect of action by the courts has been to limit the powers of local authorities and hamper their activities. Yet some decisions do favour local independence and initiative: a leading example is the Tameside case described below. A full examination of the legal position of local authorities would require an extensive review of statutes, case law and procedural technicalities. This can be found in legal textbooks and will not be attempted here. However, some analysis of the legal position is essential to an understanding of the constitutional situation of local government.

Local government law can be divided into two sections. There are branches of general law, for example, contract and tort, where special rules apply in relation to local government. A local authority cannot be held liable on an *ultra vires* contract because it had no power to make the contract in the first place. In general, a local authority is responsible for the tortious – that is, wrongful – acts of its servants. Since an authority has no power to commit torts one might expect, following the doctrine applied to contracts, that it could not be liable for wrongs done by its employees. Fortunately, in this instance, the courts have not been logical or consistent. However, there are exceptions to the general rule. If a local authority employee is acting under powers conferred on him personally by statute, the authority is not liable for his actions. Local authorities also have a wide range of powers that are not possessed by a private person, rights of entry into private premises for certain purposes, rights to destroy infected goods or unsound food, and so on. It follows that many things done by local government officers, which would be tortious acts if undertaken by private individuals, are legitimated by statute.

The other sector of local government law relates specifically to the way in which local authorities carry out their functions. Here again a twofold distinction can be made between provisions for appeals against council decisions and wider opportunities for ensuring that local authorities both keep within their powers and carry out their duties.

Magistrates' courts deal with disputes arising out of the application of building regulations and the naming of streets. County courts hear appeals against closing orders. The High Court hears appeals against compulsory purchase orders and clearance orders. This is a selection of examples, not an exhaustive list. But it must be noted that the powers of the High Court to review compulsory purchase and similar orders are very limited: any action must be started within six weeks of the order being confirmed and the court can consider an appeal only on grounds of *ultra vires* or if it is satisfied that the applicant has been 'substantially prejudiced' by some defect in the procedure when the order was being prepared and considered. The time limit is necessary to prevent local authorities being required to restore houses that have been knocked down or to return land to its previous owners after work has started on the erection of new buildings.

The sector of judicial control which offers the greatest constitutional interest is that relating to the extent of local authority powers and the way in which they are used. The principle of *ultra vires* has been described above. Here it may be useful to give an illustration of how closely the principle is applied. In *Attorney-General* v. *Fulham Corporation* (1921) the issue was whether Fulham Council had the power to run a municipal laundry. The Baths and Washhouses Acts 1846–7 gave Fulham as a public health authority, the right to provide baths and washhouses where people could wash themselves and wash clothes. The question was whether this power allowed Fulham to provide a service whereby the servants of the council would wash clothes in return for payments to the corporation. The court's answer was 'no'. A more recent example in 1981 was the decision that Hereford and Worcester were not entitled to impose a charge for musical tuition at school because such a charge would be contrary to the general provision of the Education Act 1944 that education should be free. In December 1981 the House of Lords ruled that the newly introduced system of subsidised fares on tubes and buses in London could not be justified within the terms of the London Transport Act 1969. The supplementary rate imposed by the Labour-controlled Greater London Council to meet the cost of lower fares was held to be illegal. The decision was less than clear-cut. Their Lordships ruled that the GLC had to balance the interests of the ratepayers against those of the transport users; it had not carried out this fiduciary duty in a proper manner. Since the subsidy policy had been placed before the electorate the previous May and had received popular support, their Lordships' argument may be thought unacceptable in terms of democracy. But it is the case that an election result, by itself, cannot change the law. There have been many cases of this kind in which a restrictive ruling has been given on the interpretation of local government statutes. The courts also supervise the decisions of the District Auditors in relation to *ultra vires* and unreasonable expenditure: the work of the District Auditor is considered separately in a later section of this chapter.

Judicial proceedings can be instituted to force an authority to carry out its statutory obligations: such action is now rare, but in earlier centuries there were important cases relating to the maintenance of highways and the provision of drainage.

Local authorities can also be required to observe certain rules of equitable behaviour known as the principles of 'natural justice'. The two most important are that no man shall be judge in his own cause and that no man shall be condemned unheard. If an elected member participates in the making of a decision of benefit to himself, then it can be declared void by a court. In 1933 a decision of the Hendon Rural District Council to permit the construction of a roadhouse was quashed because one of the councillors present was financially interested in the project. There are difficulties and limitations connected with these declarations of interest which were discussed in Chapter 4. The other concept, that no man shall be condemned unheard, has led to the establishment of a wide range ot public inquiries into the actions of public authorities, especially where these are likely to interfere with private property and other rights. It also governs the way in which these inquiries are conducted. The leading case here is *Errington* v. *Ministry of Health* (1935). The facts were that the Minister of Health had ordered a public inquiry into objections against a clearance order made by a local authority. The inquiry was duly held by a ministry inspector, but subsequently the inspector visited the site accompanied by local authority officials but without the objectors. This was held to constitute listening to evidence from one side in the absence of the other, so the High Court quashed the minister's decision to confirm the clearance order. It will be noted that this was not an action against a local authority, but an action against the way in which a minister had used his supervisory powers over local government.

An outstanding example of judicial control in recent years is the Tameside dispute of 1976. The Labour majority on the council made arrangements to end selection for secondary schools in 1976 and to operate a comprehensive system. However, the Conservatives won the local election a few months before the change-over was due and they were pledged to retain some grammar schools. After some preliminary negotiations with Tameside, the secretary of state, Mr Mulley, issued a direction that Tameside should give up the intention to continue selective entry to some secondary schools. This instruction was based on section 68 of the Education Act 1944 which provides that when the secretary of state is satisfied that a local education authority is acting unreasonably a direction may be issued to that authority such as appears to the secretary of state to be expedient. The language of the Act is so broad that one might have thought that Mr Mulley's action was fully justified, at least in law. Yet Tameside appealed to the courts. The case was fought up to the House of Lords where Mr Mulley lost: their Lordships held that there was no basis for the claim that Tameside was acting unreasonably. They rejected the Whitehall view that plans for comprehensive education were so far advanced that it was impractical to change them and that the difficulties of arranging a selection system in the short time available were insuperable.

Previously section 68 had been used almost entirely in personal cases where parents had appealed to the DES against a local refusal to send a child to a particular school. Its effect had been to uphold parental choice rather than to intervene on issues of policy. Now its force is in doubt. Any dispute between a local education authority and the secretary of state over what is reasonable may be referred to a court and there is clearly no guarantee that the ministerial direction will be supported. Thus the judgement of a minister responsible to Parliament can be replaced by the judgement of judges responsible to no one.

If there is disagreement over the meaning of words in a statute it is proper that the matter be settled in a court of law. To this extent, judicial control over local government is unavoidable. It remains, however an unsatisfactory process. Local authorities are responsible to the local electorate and try to serve the public interest as they think best. They are in a quite different position to the ordinary defendant in that they rarely break the law deliberately. If they do break the law, it is normally because a law is unclear or becomes unclear when lawyers start arguing about it. Another aspect of litigation is the heavy expense, so local authorities are not challenged in the courts – other than before the magistrates – unless someone is prepared to spend a substantial sum. It follows that judicial control is partial in its operation. Some parts of local government law have been heavily contested in the courts while other parts go unchallenged. The statutes that are disputed tend to be those that affect property, that is, rating, housing, compulsory purchase and town and country planning. The Tameside case noted above is untypical in the sense that the amount of recent litigation over educational administration has been small.

The merit of being able to appeal to a minister rather than a judge is cheapness. Yet we recoil from the idea that a minister should be able to interpret the law for this would place still more power in ministerial hands. There may also be a feeling that, as a dominant factor in the sphere of public administration, a minister would be biased in favour of local authorities against individuals, or would be guided by political considerations. A judge is held to be impartial and to give decisions based on recognised rules of statutory interpretation. However, since judges often find it possible to disagree, it is arguable that a judicial decision may be nothing more than the personal preference of a judge. Even so, the personal view of a judge may still be preferable to the personal view of a minister in that a judicial decision can be overruled by subsequent parliamentary discussion and action, whereas a ministerial decision is virtually irreversible in Parliament because of party loyalty and party discipline.

SUPERVISION BY WHITEHALL

Over the years the extent and purpose of central scrutiny of local affairs have changed substantially. Before 1939 the main concern was the quality of local administration. Many local authorities were small and financially weak; senior staff often lacked professional qualifications. So proposals to borrow money to finance capital spending were subject to central review to ensure that schemes were adequately prepared. Inspection was developed in the nineteenth century. Schools were visited to check on the teachers. Police inspectors from the Home Office examined the efficiency of the local constabulary. Chief constables and local medical officers of health could not be dismissed without central agreement; thus these officials were not deterred from carrying out their duties for fear of offending local people of influence. District audit was designed to ensure that accounts were properly kept and that no illegal payments were made.

Between 1939 and 1945 the business of local authorities was greatly restricted by the need to allocate resources to the war effort. After 1945 restrictions continued for two distinct reasons. Shortages caused by the war lasted for several years so the government rationed the amount of building work that local authorities could undertake. The Labour government also wished to improve standards of local services and desired greater uniformity. Indeed, the Education Act 1944, introduced by the wartime coalition government, had the same philosophy. So began the national political pressure to influence local policy, not just in particular places that showed inadequacies, but over the country as a whole. Later this process was illustrated by the Labour insistence on comprehensive secondary education and the Conservative determination that council houses be offered for sale to sitting tenants.

The major purpose now of central control is to influence the amount of local expenditure. The Cabinet assumes responsibility for overall economic policy, and local budgets are now so large that they cannot be ignored when a government draws up its programme and priorities. Both Conservative and Labour ministers accept this principle. Conservatives are more enthusiastic about the need to reduce expenditure in order to lower taxation. However, in 1976 the Labour government, faced with a balance of payments crisis and the need to seek assistance from the International Monetary Fund, also urged local authorities to prune back their estimates.

The extent of central influence varies from function to function and between different parts of a service. Whitehall departments are deeply involved in all major aspects of education, policing and town and country planning; they are less concerned with public libraries, municipal entertainments and recreational facilities. The Department of the Environment is alert to the financial aspects of housing, but does not intervene in the selection of tenants. The Department of Transport is deeply involved in major road improvements but ignores maintenance of minor roads except in the context of overall cost. These variations are caused by the uneven amount of political interest attracted to different services. Inevitably, the most expensive services command most attention.

Most of the supervisory activity by the central government is authorised specifically by statute, but there are a few examples of ministers being entrusted by Parliament with broad oversight of a particular local government function. The Local Authority Social Services Act 1970 is the most authoritarian piece of local government law to have been passed in recent years. It requires the responsible authorities to appoint a social services committee, restricts the business coming before the committee subject to the consent of the secretary of state, empowers the secretary of state to prescribe qualifications to be held by a director of social services and requires local authorities to act under general ministerial guidance in relation to these functions. The Education Act 1944 is another extreme example of conferring wide power on a minister by generalised wording. According to the Act it is the duty of the Secretary of State for Education 'to secure the effective execution by local authorities, under his control and direction, of the national policy for providing a varied and comprehensive educational service in every area'. (In view of the current controversy about comprehensive education, it must be stressed that the word 'comprehensive' in the Education Act was used in the normal sense of all-embracing, not in the recent specialised sense which implies the abolition of selection for secondary education.) The language of the Act is strong and scarcely fits the conception that local authorities should govern: rather it implies that local education authorities are mere agents to carry out a minister's will.

The Education Act 1944 is vague in another important sense. It speaks of the national policy for education without defining what the policy is to be. Presumably the policy is to be decided, and redefined from time to time, by the responsible minister. Thus the wide powers of the 1944 Act entitle the Secretary of State for Education and Science to press forward or restrain the ending of selection for secondary education depending on the viewpoint of the government.

Many other Acts give ministers a strong reserve power over local authorities. If a minister is satisfied that a council has failed to perform a particular function adequately he may be empowered to issue an order to the council to instruct it to do certain things, or he may transfer powers from a district council to a county council, or he may take over the powers himself. This default power was first incorporated in the Public Health Act 1875 in respect of sewerage and water supply but was never actually used. Similar provisions are to be found *inter alia* in the Public Health Act 1936, the Town and Country Planning Acts 1947 and 1962, the Civil Defence Act 1948 and the Housing Finance Act 1972. These certainly give ministers a big stick to brandish at recalcitrant local councils, but they are called into effect very rarely; postwar examples relate to civil defence at Coventry and St Pancras and, more recently, to housing at Clay Cross. There is no difference between the political parties in the matter of these broad statutory powers over local government: both Conservative and Labour governments have inserted default clauses into local government legislation.

One of the oldest forms of central supervision is the use of inspection, first employed by Chadwick in 1834 to review the activities of the Boards of Guardians. Four local authority services are subject to regular inspection, police, fire, education, children. There are two aspects to an inspector's duties. Primarily he has to ensure that local services are efficient and that standards are

maintained: he also advises local authorities and his own department on matters of technique and policy improvement.

The process of inspection is concerned not so much with council
policy as with the way in which council servants perform their duties.
There are other types of control over officials. In some cases
regulations prescribe their qualifications and duties. Various controls over the appointment and dismissal of local government
officers are outlined above in the section describing the role of
officials. The most exhaustive control over personnel is to be found
in the police and fire services where the Home Secretary can make
regulations governing appointment, dismissal, discipline and conditions of service. In the case of fire brigades the supervision extends
to methods of training and the provision of certain items of
equipment.

The term inspector is also used, rather misleadingly, to describe
officials who preside over various types of local inquiries. Their task
is to hear objections to proposals and report thereon to a Whitehall
department. Planning provides the major examples of this process.
Strategic long-term plans formed by county planning authorities are
submitted to a public inquiry. Appeals against refusal of development applications are similarly treated. Schemes for new airports or
motorways often arouse great controversy; on such occasions, the
public inquiry attracts much publicity. Less attention is paid to
inquiries into clearance orders where a local authority wishes to
acquire an area of sub-standard housing and perhaps other property
for the purpose of redevelopment. The Department of the Environment will send an inspector to hear objections. Other examples are
inquiries into objections into the compulsory purchase of land by
local authorities for housing, school-building, road-widening, and so
on, and disputes over footpaths. Save in minor planning cases, the
inspector does not himself make the decision. His task is to listen to
evidence presented by both sides to a dispute, normally to visit the
site in question, and make a report with a recommendation to the
appropriate minister. The minister is responsible for the final
decision and in the vast majority of cases will uphold the inspector's
opinion. Since 1958 the reports of inspectors have been published,
unless considerations of national security are involved, so it is
possible to see if the minister has overruled his inspector.

Many Acts require a minister to adjudicate in a conflict between a
local authority and an individual, but some such disputes go to a
court of law. Parliament has been careful to protect private rights
against unjustifiable interference by local government, but no clear
line can be drawn between the sort of issues that goes to a minister
and that which goes to a court. The policy imposed by Parliament

has varied. Before 1930 appeals against closing orders – that a house is unfit for human habitation – were decided by the Ministry of Health: now they go before a court.

Ministers also adjudicate in disputes between local authorities. Here there are no public inquiries; the councils concerned submit arguments on paper and the issue is decided within the Department. If education authorities are in dispute over which of them is responsible for the education of a child, the matter is determined by the Secretary of State for Education. If a similar issue arises over a child taken into care, responsibility is allocated by the Secretary of State for the Social Services. If a county council disagrees with a county district over whether a local plan is in conformity with the strategic county plan, the issue is referred to the Secretary of State for the Environment.

The wide scope of administrative control requires regular communications between local authorities and central departments. Applications from individual authorities are normally dealt with through correspondence. General guidance from Departments to local authorities comes through a variety of documents, some printed and some duplicated. Some bulletins deal with technical matters of concern to specialists. More general questions are dealt with in Circulars. Their contents vary. Some seek to promote a particular course of action while others merely provide information. Before 1979 a file of these Circulars was a good guide to contemporary developments in local government. More recently the total of Circulars has been reduced as part of the Conservative desire for economy in administration. But if Circulars are in decline, Codes of Practice flourish and they give detailed advice on how a particular administrative task should be carried out. These Codes need not come from government departments; some are generated by local government, for example, the LAMSAC guide on the protection of computerised personal data held by social services departments.

A third means of communication is through personal contact. When a council has a serious problem it may send a small deputation of councillors and officials to London to put their point of view to civil servants or perhaps even a minister. Civil servants also visit local authorities, but such visits are most often made by officials with specialised qualifications, for example, engineers, surveyors and planners. Senior civil servants, the members of the administrative class who have the greatest influence on ministry decisions, more rarely travel round local authorities. This is a possible ground of criticism. It is arguable that central control would be more flexible, that central departments would have a fuller understanding of local difficulties, if there was more personal intercourse between

Whitehall and the counties and districts. Yet it is not certain that local authorities would welcome more visits from civil servants. They are, quite rightly, jealous of their independence and would resent anything that seemed to be a call from a new type of general inspector.

For decades the local authorities have expressed concern at the vast number of detailed controls to which they are subject. They greatly increase administrative cost. They hinder local initiative. They make for difficulties in adapting national policies to local circumstances. After years of grumbling the associations of local authorities ultimately took more positive action. In 1979 they produced a *Review of Central Government Controls over Local Authorities*. The report was detailed and revealed a bureaucratic nightmare. It showed that 227 different forms dealing with financial matters had to be completed. There were a further thirty question-naires dealing with housing matters. Ministers had power to tell local councils how to control unruly bus queues or restrict the use of horses and carts. Apart from such trivia there was the more important complaint that government departments gave conflicting advice: the Treasury and the DOE counselled financial restraint while the DHSS issued guidelines which implied a need to expand services.

The newly elected Conservative government responded favour-ably to this document. It fitted well with the Conservative view that the business of government should be simplified and made cheaper. Central supervision wastes time and occupies expensive staff time in Whitehall and in local offices. So the Local Government Planning and Land Act 1980 scrapped many controls. On minor matters local authorities enjoy a little more freedom. But they do not enjoy more freedom in any fundamental sense. The Conservative method is to mould the actions of local authorities by imposing financial restraint.

Financial controls fall broadly into three categories. The process of rationing capital expenditure has been explained in the previous chapter. The rather intricate issues of audit are examined below. The third and most controversial technique is to put pressure on individual local authorities by adjusting the size of their annual grant.

The Local Government Act 1958 authorised the reduction of grant payable to any local authority which failed to provide an adequate standard of service. This power was never used. Its intention was to stimulate any council that was not spending enough. The provisions in the Local Government, Planning and Land Act 1980 have the opposite purpose: councils that spend too much are to be discouraged and penalised. Inevitably, local government objects to this system. All the associations of local authorities are unhappy. The issue is not party political; Conservative and Labour councillors agree that ministers go too far in attempting to influence local decisions. It is argued that the expenditure targets set for local authorities are unrealistic, partly because the effect of inflation is underestimated, partly because they ignore changing circumstances. In a period of recession and high unemployment the demand for services always increases. The targets for future expenditure are fixed with reference to base dates in the past; these are arbitrary in the sense that any one council might have had untypically high expenditure in the base year. The prospect is that most local authorities will fail to keep within the target set for them.

DISTRICT AUDIT

District audit requires separate treatment because it involves a unique combination of political, administrative and judicial factors. Each new category of local authority created since 1844 has had to have its accounts examined by a government-appointed auditor – now known as district auditor. Boroughs outside London were the only authorities to escape: they could choose between employing professional auditors, using district audit or choosing auditors by election – the latter method was quaintly archaic and rarely used. Except for London, the 1972 Act permitted councils to choose between district audit and professional audit, but an appointment in the latter category had to be approved by the secretary of state. Relatively few authorities took advantage of this new freedom. The district auditor must be satisfied that accounts are accurate and compiled in accordance with proper accounting principles. Any criticisms are to be included in his report to the local authority and the secretary of state.

The influence of the audit rests upon the principle of *ultra vires* which requires local authorities to be able to produce legal authorisation for all their actions. The principle was not imposed on local government by a deliberate act of national policy; it evolved from judicial decisions which limited the activities of railway companies to business directly connected with the running of a railway. The argument was that railways were authorised by Acts of Parliament and, as statutory corporations, they must be restricted to the purposes for which they were created. Local authorities were immediately involved because they are all statutory corporations, apart from boroughs outside London. Whether provincial boroughs were also governed by the *ultra vires* rule has become a wholly academic question since, under the 1972 Act, all local authorities are statutory authorities. So local government is fettered by a legal rule that has not received specific authorisation from Parliament: it is, moreover, a rule that the courts have interpreted very strictly.

There can, of course, be two views on the desirability of the *ultra vires* principle. Certainly, it inhibits enterprise and experiment; it also removes opportunities for extravagance and folly. Were councils freed from this restraint they would still be subject to the ballot-box and if electors were not satisfied by the reasons offered for inflated rate-demands a change of councillors and council policy would become highly likely. A few adventures or misadventures by local authorities could rapidly reduce public apathy about their activities. One has the feeling, however, that the *ultra vires* principle is now widely accepted by ministers, Parliament, local officials and councillors with a certain sense of relief in that it prevents unorthodoxy and fresh difficulties. Optional activities are normally those which cause the greatest friction, partly because they provide obvious targets in any economy drive and partly because their continuation depends wholly on the will of the local council, and there is no possibility of pushing off responsibility on to the central government. Some local disputes about cultural expenditure have attracted widespread publicity. In the 1920s Labour Members of Parliament supported a Local Authorities (Enabling) Bill which sought to give larger local authorities discretionary powers to promote trading and cultural activities. Yet subsequent Labour governments have shown no enthusiasm whatever for this sort of legislation. The issue seemed to be dead. However, the 1972 Act allows a local authority, other than a parish meeting, to incur expenditure up to a rate of two new pence for any purpose which in its opinion would benefit its area, provided that such activity is not subject to other statutory provisions. The restraint of *ultra vires* has been weakened by this new element of flexibility: yet the extent of the freedom is steadily eroded by inflation combined with the failure to reassess property for rating purposes.

The Maud Committee suggested that a further relaxation be allowed so that local authorities be given a 'general competence' to do whatever they feel to be in the interests of their areas, subject to not encroaching on the spheres of other public bodies and to 'appropriate safeguards for the protection of public and private interests'. The proposal appeared radical but was also extremely vague. The idea of safeguarding private interests could inhibit any scheme to undertake commercial activities; even cultural and recreational provision could conflict with existing business interests. There would also be widespread objection to any right to subsidise local political or religious organisations. However, some foreign countries do have 'general competence' clauses. The idea has obvious attractions and could do much to enliven local government. But there are great difficulties in the way of giving this plan a precise legal form and it was not included in the 1972 Act.

Accounts of a local authority are open for public inspection. An aggrieved resident may challenge any item of expenditure and submit his objection to the auditor. If the auditor does not uphold the objection he may be required within a period of six weeks to give reasons for his decision. The objector may then take his case to the courts. Since 1972 district audit has not been empowered to impose penalties; it has to ask a court of law to do so. The court may surcharge those held responsible for illegal expenditure. If the amount involved exceeds £2,000 those concerned may be disqualified for a period from being councillors; this penalty may be remitted if the court believes that the councillors had thought the expenditure to be lawful.

The traditional objection to district audit has been that it empowered a government official – albeit one independent of ministers and exercising a quasi-judicial function – to impose penalties on elected representatives for using their judgement on how best to serve the interests of their electors. And surcharges were not merely on illegal expenditure but on expenditure held to be unreasonable. Between 1930 and 1980 district audit was not involved in policy confrontations with elected councillors. There may have been private warnings that certain expenditure is questionable and should not be repeated, but legal action has been avoided. District audit can still criticise publicly the financial policy of a council: such a report could conceivably encourage a ratepayer to take the authority to court on the ground that certain action was *ultra vires*.

Reform of the audit system has become a live political issue. The Layfield Report urged that district audit should do more to improve the efficiency of local administration; this topic is examined in Chapter 7. In 1981 the Public Accounts Committee of the House of Commons proposed that the Comptroller and Auditor General (the parliamentary official in charge of the scrutiny of central government accounts) should assume responsibility for district audit. The consequence would be that the Public Accounts Committee could then itself conduct inquiries into the financial affairs of local authorities. All the associations of local authorities strongly opposed such a move on the ground that it would further erode the independence of local government. The government accepted that such an arrangement would be inconsistent with the constitutional position of local authorities. Instead, the intention is to establish a new Audit Commission appointed by the Secretaries of State for the Environment and for Wales from persons with relevant expertise from industry, commerce and the professions together with representatives from local government. The new Commission is to take over the existing district auditors and will also use auditors from private firms. Local authorities lose the right to choose their own auditors. The Audit Commission can undertake studies designed to promote value for money in local administration and there can be some overlap with the work of LAMSAC. The use of auditors from the private sector is intended to feed new blood into the system; it can be argued that the relationship between district audit staff and local government has become too steady, too regular and too cosy. Another aspect of the shake-up is that district auditors are moved from the DoE to a new quango. This transfer could imply greater independence from Whitehall. In fact, district audit has traditionally occupied a quasi-judicial role and did not receive ministerial instructions in relation to the business of individual local authorities.

Meanwhile, the question emerges, will an invigorated audit system become involved in policy clashes with local authorities?

CENTRAL–LOCAL RELATIONS

There is no generally accepted theory of central–local relationships. Two contrasting patterns are regularly promoted. One is a partnership of colleagues in a joint enterprise; the other is a principal/agent arrangement in which local authorities act at the behest of their national masters. Both patterns illustrate an aspect of the truth. Local services are organised by the local councils; without their co-operation the central government could not ensure the smooth running of these services, at least in the short run. Again, ministers are usually willing to listen to advice from local authorities because of their practical experience and knowledge of local conditions. On the other hand, local councils depend for their powers on national legislation and some local government law is certainly shaped on the principal and agent framework, notably the provisions for education and the social services. Ministers tend to speak in terms of partnership when they want to be tactful and in terms of principal and agent whenever they wish to enforce a particular policy.

The development of political controversy in relation to local affairs has also tended to link central and local government more closely together. This is not simply a matter of national parties contesting local elections or of the control of a council's policy by the 'caucus' of the local majority party. In the past ministers have often claimed political credit for the activities of local authorities, especially in connection with building houses and schools, in spite of the fact that a large part of this construction has been carried out by councils dominated by their political opponents.

It is often argued that such ministerial influence is undemocratic in that the wishes of locally elected representatives can be overridden by the edict of a remote organisation in Whitehall. Yet this argument is not easy to sustain. If democracy is defined as the acceptance of majority opinion, it would seem to be as democratic to follow the will of the minister who represents the national majority as it is to follow the wishes of those who represent but a local majority. If democracy is defined in terms of paying attention to local opinion, then the smaller the unit of opinion the more attention should be paid to its desires. Should a parish council be allowed to override a county council? Should the representatives of a ward be entitled to insist that a different policy be applied to their ward as opposed to the other wards in the borough? Financial considerations apart, claims of this sort are a prescription for anarchy. Here is a dilemma. A healthy democracy needs strong, vigorous and independent-minded local government genuinely able to exercise initiative and judgement. At the same time local authorities get massive monetary aid from the Treasury and are expected to assist in promoting national social purposes.

These theoretical considerations can be illustrated by two examples, selection for secondary education and the sale of council houses. Both these issues have entered the national political arena. In both cases there are two aspects to the question; what is the best policy and how should decisions be made – by the national government or by the local authority? Inevitably, when a party puts a policy in its manifesto for a general election, it will, if it wins, claim a mandate to impose its solution. Thus Labour wants to abolish the 11+ examination and Conservatives want to insist on the sale of council houses. Policy fluctuates, depending upon which party won the last general election. Yet a distinction can be drawn between the two issues. If it can be shown that a selection examination works badly, because it produces inaccurate assessment of individuals and is socially divisive, then those conclusions apply to the country as a whole. Arguments about the sale of council houses are more varied. Some are ideological: that property ownership encourages a greater sense of independence and responsibility. Some are local; that an area has an acute shortage of accommodation or that an agricultural community will disintegrate if council houses become holiday homes. Where local conditions vary, the case for local decision becomes stronger. But that is not a conclusion that national politicians are likely to welcome.

When the national government denies discretion to local authorities, local government becomes merely local administration. Such a process must cause intense frustration where a majority of councillors are opposed to the national policy. They can claim that they have a local popular mandate which they are required to ignore. Does this make local democracy a farce?

The independence of local authorities has been deeply undermined by their reliance on financial help from the central government. The rating system is now under such severe attack that its continued existence is uncertain. There is no doubt that local rates are a most unsatisfactory form of taxation for there is no certain correlation, as there is with income tax, between the amount an individual has to pay and his capacity to pay. Resistance to paying higher rates, aggravated by the unfairness of the system, has effectively reduced the taxing capacity of local councils and has led to incessant demands for more state subsidies. It is widely argued that education – easily the most expensive local government service – is a national service and, as such, should be financed entirely by the national Exchequer. Yet how far would it continue to be a local government service if education authorities had no financial responsibility save to the Secretary of State for Education? Meanwhile, local control of administration and expenditure, albeit constrained by Whitehall, does preserve an element of community responsibility, pride and satisfaction. Services provided by the central government do not inspire similar attitudes. Compare the health service to local welfare services. There is general dissatisfaction with the hospital service – not necessarily with the individual contributions of doctors, nurses and hospital administrators, but with the scale of provision as a whole. There is a feeling that 'they', the anonymous, abstract and unknown controllers of the system, ought to effect various improvements. Controllers of the local welfare services are not unknown; if there are serious complaints, they will soon hear of them. Where cost is the obstacle to meeting the complaint, the difficulty is more readily appreciated. 'To improve the welfare services means putting the rate up' is a statement which carries a more meaningful choice than 'To improve hospitals means an increase in taxation'. It is not merely that the national purse may appear bottomless, it is also the case that any successful local claim on national resources has a net benefit to the local community. So long as cost is linked to a local tax, the cost–benefit relationship is realistic. Whenever the government takes over a local service it puts a premium on grumbling by destroying local financial responsibility.

Further, the nineteenth-century desire to achieve minimum standards throughout the country in relation to vital services such as poor relief and education has tended to develop into the imposition of maximum standards and, indeed, to an overall regime of uniformity. As local authorities receive so much financial aid this equality of provision is easily justified on grounds of fair distribution of the national taxpayer's money.

The status of local government has been eroded in this century both by local weakness and by the development of a highly centralised form of public administration. Local weakness is financial and also a matter of organisation and personnel. The traditional committee system was better designed for promoting discussion than for promoting leadership. The reformed structure and streamlined committee organisation will make for improvement but they also impose a heavy burden on many councillors, especially committee chairmen. Some chairmen have the necessary time, ability and vigour to take full command of the business of their committees. Others – probably a majority – lack one or more of these essential qualities. With chief officers increasingly conditioned to think in terms of efficient management rather than adventurous policies, it is almost inevitable that, with exceptions, local councils conform to a national trend and do not take exciting initiatives. Meanwhile the advantage of the central government is the product of powerful interlocking factors: a country that is densely populated but relatively small in area; the cultural, financial and political supremacy of London; the firmly entrenched two-party system that gives the Cabinet a secure parliamentary majority; the acceptance by both parties of welfare policies which they are determined to control nationally.

There is a case for urging that these centripetal forces should be resisted. Strong reasons can be advanced against national intervention in local affairs, notably on matters of detail. Every increase in central control requires more staff in national offices to check what local authorities are doing. Not merely does this cost money but it adds to delay. Each new item in the catalogue of supervision means a further loss of local responsibility. Both councillors and local government officers can plead with some justification that it is not their fault is something goes amiss since they are acting under central direction. Distant control must be frustrating. It can develop a feeling among vigorous and able people that service in local government as elected representatives or salaried officers is not worthwhile.

The Layfield Committee's inquiry into local government finance stressed the effect on central–local relationships caused by the financial weakness of local councils. The report expressed concern about the confusion caused by a clear lack of accountability for local authority expenditure. Most local spending is directly related to some statutory obligation imposed by central government. The whole Layfield Report is based on the theme of accountability: it argues that those responsible for causing expenditure should accept the onus of finding the money to meet the bills. If present trends continued this would require central government to accept responsibility for the bulk of local expenditure. Ministers would have to determine broadly how much local authorities should spend and for what purpose. Ministers would provide grants and would also indicate the rate poundage necessary to finance appropriate standards of local service. Some local discretion would still remain. Thus local authorities could provide a better standard of service than that required by central government; for this purpose the local rate would be raised above the level required by central government. Councillors would be responsible for the discretionary element in the rate levy to the local electorate; they would be accountable to the minister for the efficient conduct of the non-discretionary expenditure.

The Layfield Committee were not happy with the prospect of such developments. They preferred an alternative in which local councils would be free to make their own spending and taxing decisions. Even so, it was admitted that central government would need, in the interests of national economic management, to supervise the total of local spending. (Whether this could be done without interference on matters of detail is questionable.) Certainly, local councils could not attain such financial autonomy without fresh taxing powers. To give them such independence, the Layfield Report proposed the introduction of a local income tax.

To give extra taxing powers to local authorities could damage the ability of the government to manage the national economy as it wished. From this standpoint, the objections to local income tax are particularly strong. Ministers want to be in control of financial policy, whichever political party is in power. If the Cabinet wants incomes restraint, local government must follow suit when making wage and salary settlements. If the Cabinet wants lower public expenditure and lower taxation, local authorities will be under strong pressure to conform. When local authorities make decisions that conflict with the economic objectives of the government, there is likely to be a clash. No government is likely to introduce reforms which would make it easier for local government to frustrate its wishes.

When the national policy is to reduce spending – and when there is a willingness to increase it – ministers will have strong views about how the changes should be made. The most convenient way to trim back is to cut capital projects rather than current expenditure. This is a natural reaction because new construction implies some improvement of service while a cut in current expenditure normally means a lowering of existing standards. If the choice is between fresh ventures and the preservation of what has already been achieved, then the latter may seem the more prudent course of action. Yet the axe falls on capital schemes also because this alternative avoids redundancy for local authority staff and thus avoids trouble with trade unions. The result is some lack of flexibility of local policy which may prevent the optimum use of resources. New needs can be sacrificed for past needs that are no longer as strong as they once were.

Further, the concept that the flow of capital works can be turned off and on like a tap – to suit the contemporary economic climate – suffers from serious limitations. Construction plans take time to prepare – planning inquiries and compulsory purchase orders may be involved. Construction works take time to complete. So it is impossible to commence projects that are not ready to start; it is wasteful to slow down or stop projects that are nearing completion. Capital programmes are now worked out two or three years in advance and acquire a momentum of their own. So if the intention is to save money immediately, current expenditure cannot escape. Here again there is a basic choice. One way forward is to trim all items a little in every budget. The other is to eliminate entirely some particular cost. The former alternative ensures that nothing dramatic takes place. Staff economies can come from natural wastage; redundancy is avoided. All services continue and it is hoped that there will be little effect on quality. Perhaps more efficient organisation can ensure that everything will continue as well as before. The second method – to stop something – is more painful. Affected interests will protest. Some people lose their jobs. Trade unions are up in arms. If fresh legislation is needed, there can be serious political difficulty. In 1979 the new Conservative government decided to end free transport for pupils who lived a long way from school. Substantial opposition came both from rural areas and from the Roman Catholic Church which feared that parents might move their children to state schools nearer their homes. The government's plan was defeated in the House of Lords and then dropped. Clearly, it is easier to make marginal adjustments all round than to insist on policy changes that stir the passions.

The difficulty is that, at some stage, the technique of marginal economies creates major trouble. There is a limit to how far it can be repeated. If routine maintenance work on buildings or equipment is postponed, in the end there must be serious damage. If administrative and secretarial staff are run down, work will be subject to delay or not done at all. If there are fewer staff and poorer facilities in residential homes, the quality of the service must fall. A system of planning controls becomes unsatisfactory if there is inadequate staff to enforce the decisions made. So the favoured means of cutting cost by trimming a little everywhere makes local government threadbare. Then the threadbare patches develop holes. That is the logical consequence of the way central government is pushing local government. If it be accepted that economies must be made, is it better to take unpleasant decisions that eliminate some activities in order to ensure that other, more essential services can maintain their standards?

In the recent past there has been some controversy over the effectiveness of central control. A picture of local government in which any initiative is crushed by the centre is perhaps an exaggeration. As local elections have become more political, the element of party organisation on councils has increased; as many authorities are controlled by political opponents of the government there will always be some resistance to Whitehall. Further, it can be argued that the variations in expenditure on local services indicate that the quality of service provision is far from uniform. It is this feeling that local authorities are still too independent that has led the conservative government to take even stronger action to try and make councillors conform to ministerial wishes. Thus legislation is introduced, as described in Chapter 5, to limit rate increases.

Why do ministers concern themselves so much with the detail of local affairs? The fashionable view that such intervention is essential to carry out national economic priorities is open to challenge. It would be quite possible to operate a simplified scheme of financial management in which the central government fixed a borrowing limit and the grant payable to each local authority. If the councillors wanted to spend more, ratepayers would have to pay more; if ratepayers objected, they could elect different councillors. This is the traditional process of democratic accountability and is much simpler and cheaper than supervision by referendum. It may be claimed that control of public spending is vital to check inflation. But on the model set out above, local borrowing would be subject to a limit imposed from above and all extra local spending would be financed from rates. Spending, financed by taxation, cannot be inflationary unless it increases demand for scarce resources. In the present situation of mass unemployment and under-use of industrial capacity, resources are not scarce but, instead, are standing idle.

No doubt, ministers intervene because they feel big and powerful; they want things to be run their way. But there is still a political cost to be paid as intervention in local affairs tends to be unpopular. It would be less damaging for ministers if they stood aside from local rows over financial and other matters. Responsibility for what was done or not done would then rest firmly at the local town or county hall.

Chapter 7

THE QUEST FOR EFFICIENCY

The need for efficiency in local government has attracted much public discussion. Indeed, the subject has been ventilated more vigorously than the parallel need for cost-effectiveness in central government. That does not mean that local administration is more wasteful. Rather the explanation is that local affairs are more visible and more vulnerable. Councillors will have more detailed information about local business than ministers can have about their departments. And national politicians may find it suits party advantage to criticise alleged local extravagance. If it so chooses, central government can institute an inquiry into local administration: councillors are not in a position to instigate a similar inquiry into the Civil Service.

Three official reports have stimulated ideas on the best way to organise the business of local authorities. In 1964 the Minister of Housing and Local Government appointed two committees of inquiry at the request of the main associations of local authorities. One committee, with Sir George Mallaby as chairman, was required to investigate the staffing of local government. The other had wider terms of reference: 'to consider in the light of modern conditions how local government might best continue to attract and retain people (both elected representatives and principal officers) of the calibre necessary to ensure its maximum effectiveness'. Under the guidance of its chairman Sir John Maud (now Lord Redcliffe-Maud) this committee undertook a far-reaching investigation into the management of local authorities. Both committees reported in 1967 and these important documents will be discussed more fully below. The mere fact that these two inquiries were set in motion did indicate a widespread malaise about local government: indeed, the terms of reference clearly imply concern about the quality of the people in local government. No great institutions can be efficient if those who work for it have limited ability or poor morale and if the public 'image' of the institution deters other most suitable persons from coming forward to help with the work. The Maud Committee proposed fundamental reforms in the internal organisation of local authorities because it felt that if councillors and officials were frustrated by petty and time-wasting methods of doing business, then able people would be less willing to concern themselves with the management of local public affairs.

The third report came from a committee set up in 1971 as a joint venture by the DoE and the four local authority associations to advise upon management arrangements for the new authorities to be created in the major reform of structure then in prospect. A steering committee was formed under the chairmanship of Sir Frank Marshall and consisted largely of representatives of the associations: the detailed recommendations were produced by a working group headed by Mr Bains, Clerk of the Kent County Council. This latter body, with a single exception, was made up of senior local government officers. The document they produced will be referred to below as the Bains Report. But the main difference between the Bains Committee and the earlier Maud and Mallaby inquiries was that it had an immediate and precise task – to try and discover how the imminent changes could be made to work to the best advantage. Maud and Mallaby, operating with a more flexible time-scale, had to try to educate local government opinion on the need for change in the traditional *modus operandi*.

Apart from new ideas on management and establishment work, local administration has been greatly affected by the onward march of technology. Sophisticated equipment replaces men and women. Much routine office work is taken over by computers. The staff are called upon to learn fresh skills. New concepts in accountancy and new applications of mathematics are used to produce material which forms a better base for making decisions. This chapter outlines the various approaches to the task of making local government more efficient.

PERSONNEL MANAGEMENT

The officers of local authorities do not constitute a single body, such as the Civil Service, employed by one master. Each authority determines its own establishment of staff and appoints its own officials. Except in the few instances where appointment or dismissal is subject to ministerial consent, and in the few cases in which there is some central prescription of qualifications, each authority is free to recruit its own officers in its own way, and to impose what qualifications it desires. Nevertheless, the whole body of local government officers possesses many uniform characteristics and in recent years has conformed increasingly to standards and uniformities introduced into pay, service conditions, entry and promotion tests, and other elements in the officer's contract of service with his employing authority. These developments are due, partly to trade union organisation among the staffs themselves, and partly to joint organisation of both the staffs and the local authorities in Whitley machinery for collective bargaining. The local government officers trade union NALGO persuaded Parliament to pass legislation in 1937 to establish a unified superannuation scheme for local government. This facilitated the movement of officers between authorities, opened up better promotion prospects and enabled officers to acquire a wider range of experience. In the interwar period NALGO also struggled hard to establish Whitley machinery, that is, to create joint consultation with employers over questions of pay and conditions of service. While such consultation was operative in some areas, it was not until 1944 that a National Joint Council was established with the agreement of the associations of local authorities. The National Joint Council is supplemented by Provincial Councils which deal with local problems. In 1946 the NJC approved a national scheme of salaries and service conditions, known as 'the charter', providing a framework of scales for the grading of posts. This is now operative throughout the country and it has been supplemented by agreements for standard gradings among certain classes of officer. Other negotiating committees have agreed upon scales of pay and standard conditions of service for the Chief Officers of local authorities.

The Whitley machinery also became responsible for setting standards of recruitment, training and qualification. It enlisted the help of university staff, the governing bodies of the professions and the various occupational groups of the service in deciding the standards to be enforced. This policy was implemented by the NJC through the establishment, under its auspices, of a Local Government Examinations Board. This Board has advisory functions on questions of education, qualifications and training and also organised examinations, the syllabuses for which concentrated on government and administration. Success at these examinations (or in obtaining equivalent qualifications offered by professional bodies) became a prerequisite, but not a guarantee, of advancing beyond certain grades in the local government hierarchy. Local government is now open to the criticism that it is examination ridden. Yet this emphasis on paper qualifications has ensured a high level of professional competence among officials. It has also done much to eliminate canvassing or corruption in the making of local appointments.

The arrangements for recruitment and training worked tolerably well until the 1960s when an increasing percentage of the more able school-leavers took various higher education courses rather than seeking immediate employment. The traditional source of recruitment to local authorities became less satisfactory. Local government looked set to lose its share of young talent unless some of those who had moved on to gain higher qualifications could be still attracted to local administration. It was feared that local government fared badly in competition with other employers because its 'image' seemed dull and uninspiring. This is not to assert that local government was or is dull and uninspiring. Like beauty, the image of local government is in the eye of the beholder.

Essentially this is the situation that faced the Mallaby Committee. Its central recommendations were predictable. Local authorities should improve their liaison arrangements with schools to show school-leavers that local administration offers an attractive and worthwhile career. Also they must recruit more university graduates and make the best possible use of the abilities of their staff. So the Mallaby Committee proposed various developments in post-entry training for staff, ranging from induction training for junior entrants to management training for senior staff. At the local level the Clerk of the authority should have an overall responsibility for establishment work including training; at the national level the committee proposed the creation of a Local Government Training Board which should both exercise some general supervision over the nature of training and also provide a central organisation which would enable local authorities to pool the cost. The associations of local authorities accepted this recommendation immediately. The Local Government Training Board was established in 1968 and also incorporated the work of the Local Government Examinations Board.

One of the Mallaby recommendations was undeniably controversial – that local authorities should provide a career structure for lay administrative officers which would take them up to the second- or third-tier position in a local authority department. The use of the term 'lay administrative officer' is curious and potentially misleading; in normal usage, a 'lay' member of a local authority is thought to be an elected representative. The Mallaby Committee thought of a 'lay' officer as one who had not obtained a specialised professional qualification but who, instead, had obtained a broad education at a university or had gained a non-technical qualification in public administration. There is a clear analogy here with the general administrators who occupy the most senior posts in the Civil Service. The 1972 Bains Report took a different view. It asserted that local government could obtain staff through the professions who would provide the necessary leadership in management.

The conflicting proposals raise the long-standing argument over the value of general education as opposed to specialised qualifications. Does a training confined to law, accountancy, engineering, or medicine narrow the mind and so render men less able to carry out managerial functions? Is the man lacking specialised knowledge so much in the hands of specialists when dealing with practical problems as to be unable to provide effective leadership? The arguments are familiar. However, it is too often overlooked that the ability to administer, to make people work together as a team, to know when to use initiative and when to be cautious, to carry responsibility squarely but not too heavily – all these are functions of aptitude and personality, the development of which is perhaps but slightly affected by the subjects a person studies. If our senior civil servants are excellent administrators, is this because of the nature of their academic studies at Oxbridge or because they gained great benefit from the Oxbridge environment in their formative years?

The Mallaby Report had little effect on the promotion policy of local authorities. The idea that senior officers in each department should have the appropriate professional or technical qualifications is now deeply engrained in local government. It is arguable that the work of local authorities differs significantly from that of central government for it is executive rather than administrative. Our local councils do not produce general rule systems for the nation at large; they carry out a range of specific duties which require differing types of expertise. Meanwhile the professional associations have become more concerned about post-qualification training, especially in the fields of administration and management. The new generation of specialised graduate entrants will thus be better equipped to undertake higher administrative duties. In these circumstances the outlook for the lay administrative officer is not bright.

The 1974 remapping of areas cannot fail to have had an impact on the prospects of local government officers. Fewer authorities with larger departments must reduce the chances of an individual reaching the level of chief officer or a deputy. Again, if there are fewer separate employers, the opportunities to move from one authority to another must be diminished. If departments are larger there may be a greater tendency for middle-ranking posts to be filled by internal promotion. Able and ambitious officers at third- and fourth-tier rank are likely to experience growing frustration as the years go by.

To turn to the national level, no action has been taken to institute a Central Staffing Organisation as recommended by the Mallaby Committee. However, the Consultative Council on Local Government Finance is fully conscious of the need to promote the efficient use of staff and the local authority associations are alert to the manpower implications of the administration of services. Meanwhile there are three national bodies concerned in various ways with local government staff – the LGTB (Local Government Training Board) and LAMSAC (Local Authorities Management Services Advisory Committee). There would be a simplification of machinery if these bodies could be united into one. Yet there are great obstacles in the way. In particular, the unions have a different role in each of these organisations. They nominate members of LGTB; they negotiate with LACSAB; they are held at arms' length by LAMSAC. And as long as local authorities jealously maintain the status of independent and individual employers it will be impossible to move far with the development of national personnel policies.

Training is essentially the responsibility of each local authority. It covers, or should cover, all classes of employee – not only clerical and administrative staff. The role of the Local Government Training Board is to identify and assess training needs, advise councils on how best these needs can be met and provide a service to support the efforts of the local authorities. Initially, the Board had the task of persuading councils to devote resources to this work; now training systems are well established and this missionary role is fading. Its main function has become the provision of training material together with a limited advisory service which offers stimulus and encouragement. The role of the Board in connection with examinations is also reduced as, increasingly, local government officers study for the qualifications of professional bodies and other examining organisations. Finance for the Board is obtained by a deduction from the government grant to local authorities, the amount of this allocation being agreed by their national associations.

Compared with the era of reorganisation in the early 1970s, the problems of personnel management have today a different character. The emphasis is less on recruitment and training. Higher levels of unemployment ease the problem of attracting staff of good quality. In turn, the higher quality of staff reduces the stress on the need for training. Economy has become the dominant aim. The Local Government Manpower Watch, operated through Whitehall, issues quarterly figures showing the number of staff employed by local authorities. The intention is to put steady pressure on local government to prune back its activities and there is little doubt that the Manpower Watch statistics do provide a significant psychological weapon.

So personnel officers are concerned with trying to arrange retrenchment as smoothly as possible. A main objective is to avoid compulsory redundancy and to evade friction with the trade unions. The unions involved with local government have become stronger and more militant; the staff have been irritated by national policies of pay restraint and the traditional sense of job security is in danger of being undermined. However, in relation to cutting down jobs there should be less difficulty with the secretarial staff as the labour turnover is high and the necessary adjustments can be made by failing to fill some vacancies. Some administrative and professional staff are being encouraged to retire early and are not always replaced. To contract an organisation must be a painful process which demands much patience and tact. Difficulties arise at two levels. There are problems of individuals which may be eased by sympathetic and flexible treatment. But perhaps the greater problem is the morale of the service as a whole. The atmosphere has changed quite dramatically from the fairly optimistic days of 1974: hope of expansion of services has largely disappeared. Inevitably morale has suffered as expectations for the future drain away. The best solution can be to encourage frank discussion of the contemporary prospects for local government so that the staff adjust to the fresh situation.

CO-ORDINATION OF POLICY AND ADMINISTRATION

To be efficient an organisation must work together as a whole. If separate units are allowed to go their own way, the result must be duplication, confusion over priorities and mismanagement. This theory is everywhere accepted. How can it be applied to local government?

There are two aspects of this problem – the need to co-ordinate the work of councillors and the need to co-ordinate the activities of departments and officials. Increasingly the decisions of councillors are harmonised by the party system. The majority group determines the major issues coming before a council. But there is still a need for a committee system which will permit the discussion of problems and alternative solutions and which will also ensure that decisions are put into effect.

How is the work of officials to be co-ordinated? The traditional answer has been through the Clerk of the council. A succession of official reports urged this solution in varying terms. The Royal Commission on Local Government recommended in 1929 that the Clerk was the most suitable officer to achieve co-ordination and suggested that his ability to perform this task would depend on his personality. It did not propose that the Clerk be put in a position to give instructions to other chief officers. In 1934 the Hadow Committee on the Recruitment, Training and Promotion of Local Government Officers thought that the essential qualification of a

Clerk was administrative ability. This view naturally opens up the argument whether a Clerk should necessarily have legal qualifications. The Treasury O and M Report on Coventry in 1953 again laid heavy emphasis on the administrative role of the Clerk; he should give continual consideration to measures which would achieve economies and be responsible for establishment work and an organisation and methods service. This type of recommendation involves a very real difficulty. If the Clerk is to have an overall reponsibility for the effective operation of all his council's activities, then he must be put in a position of seniority over other chief officers so that he is able, when necessary, to insist that they accept measures he feels requisite to improve efficiency. Naturally this involves some down-grading, some loss of independence, by other heads of departments and some change in the traditional practice that a chief officer is responsible to the council through his committee. Without some loss of departmental independence there can be no guarantee that a local authority's administration is an effective unity. The Maud Report, *Management of Local Government*, also stressed firmly that the Clerk should be the undisputed head of the council's staff. Since the legal profession is not the sole source of leadership ability and management acumen, it accepted also that the Clerk need not be a lawyer. The Bains Report in 1972 again argued for a single official at the top of the administrative hierarchy, and it suggested a new title – the Chief Executive.

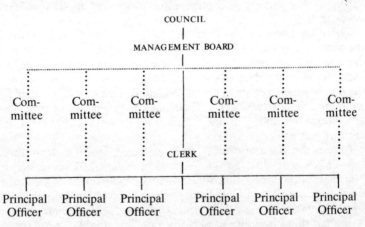

The Maud Committee Report in 1967 produced a comprehensive plan to ensure co-ordination of both administration and policy in local authorities, which involved a drastic reappraisal of the nature of committee work and the structure of local administration. A diagram illustrating the essence of the Maud proposals is given above. The core of this scheme was that each council should appoint a 'management board' consisting of between five and nine members of the council. The management board would formulate major policies and present them for approval to the council; it would have overall responsibility for the execution of these policies; it would take decisions on matters which exceeded the authority of chief officers; it would recommend proposals to the council on items which exceeded its own delegated powers. The Clerk would be responsible to the management board and through it to the council; he would also be the undisputed head of the whole of the staff. The heads of departments would be answerable to the Clerk and *not* to any committee. Obviously this plan provides unity and centralisation of decision-making achieved by down-grading all principal officers other than the Clerk and by down-grading all committees in relation to the management board. Thus in the diagram the unbroken lines indicate chains of command and the broken lines are channels of advice. The Maud Committee was specific about the new role of committees: 'Committees should not be directing or controlling bodies nor should they be concerned with routine administration.' What then are the committees to do? They would make recommendations to the management board on 'major objectives' and study how these could best be carried out. They would review progress in the sphere of the particular service that concerned them, consider reactions of the public and deal with any matters referred to them by the management board. Executive decisions would only be made in exceptional circumstances and when the management board required this to be done; the implication is that delegated authority would normally be given to officers rather than committees. The scheme also permitted a committee to consider any matter raised by its own members, but this seems to conflict with the principle noted above that committees would not consider routine administration.

Not one local authority accepted the Maud scheme *in toto*. Yet many were stimulated to streamline their committee structures and to nominate one or more major co-ordinating committees. If the idea of the management board went beyond what was currently acceptable in local government circles, it also had an important educational effect and helped to pave the way for the rather less radical Bains Report of 1972. Largely because of Maud, the Bains Committee worked within a situation where the need for reform in administrative methods was already widely accepted.

The Bains Report was more flexible in its approach to management structures: it agreed that there was no ideal model on which a local authority should operate. It argued that the functions of councillors and officials were not separable into watertight compartments and that the nature of a councillor's interest in administration also varied between individuals. Some were mainly attracted to welfare work; others to restricting expenditure; others to management, often on commercial lines; others in general service to the community. The Report added 'Other categories can no doubt be identified', but was too tactful to proceed further. It follows from this analysis that councillors will want to fill different roles in their public duties. Some are keen to be involved in major questions of policy, resource allocation and management. Others are content to be occupied with more detailed committee work.

The report followed what has become normal doctrine in urging that a local authority should have a senior or central committee, advised by a Chief Executive, to formulate policy on major issues and generally oversee all the authority's activities. Unlike the Maud management board, the Bains central policy committee was not to have a monopoly of policy-making because some decisions were to be left with functional committees. A central policy committee should frame a comprehensive plan to govern priorities in expenditure which should be revised regularly. It was important that previous decisions should not be regarded as immutable. The report stressed that more attention should be paid to the effectiveness of local government services: in the past tools of measurement had concentrated on expenditure, on input into a service, rather than its output. This prescription is splendid in theory. Yet how can it be applied in practice? Education is the most expensive local function: here is the greatest opportunity to check efficiency by improving output. But how do you measure output of a school or college – by examination results? Any attempt to proceed on these lines would be reminiscent of the 1860s: it would invoke overwhelming opposition from educationalists. Output of clerical and manual employees engaged on mainly routine tasks can be subjected to some form of measurement, but to apply similar checks to professional and managerial staffs cannot adequately assess, and would probably damage, the *quality* of their work. The Bains Committee did not really face up to these problems. Its keenness to promote efficiency at the very highest levels of administration is still praiseworthy. There was to be no soft or quiet life for those in top jobs. It doubted whether every chief officer needed a deputy. And it produced the radical notion that chief officials should be subject to an annual appraisal of their performance by a sub-committee of the policy committee advised by the Chief Executive; the latter should be similarly appraised by the policy committee itself.

A central Policy and Resources Committee was the main feature of the Bains model for local authority management. Four sub-committees were also recommended to deal with finance, staff, land and a general review of performance in relation to objectives. It was emphasised that these sub-committees should not concern themselves with trivial questions of expenditure but should think in broad terms about major issues. The Policy Committee should not consist solely of chairmen of other committees; it should include 'back-bench' councillors and some drawn from political minorities. So it would not be so much of a Cabinet as the Maud-style management board. There would be a less sharp distinction between inner-group councillors who serve on the Policy Committee and those who do not. The pattern of other committees should be related to the objectives of a council rather than to the organisation of particular services: thus committee structure need not follow departmental structure. When major decisions have to be made, committees should consider alternative means of reaching their objectives. Not surprisingly the Bains Report saw no virtue in area sub-committees operating within a scheme of delegated authority, for such bodies do not assist managerial efficiency. However, where an authority covers a wide area of countryside, there is likely to be pressure, not merely for decentralised access to services, but also for decentralised decisions so that county administration can become more sensitive to local needs and opinion. The report did accept that, in some cases, services would have to operate through local offices and it recommended that such offices should cover areas which corresponded with district council boundaries.

The Bains Committee saw no need to insist that the Chief Executive should have any specific qualification: this recommendation leaves the field for recruitment wide open. Nor, the Bains Report argued, should he have an official deputy – a proposal that invites an awkward hiatus if the Chief Executive should become ill, die, resign, or otherwise disappear. The intention was the the Chief Executive should have no specific departmental responsibilities so that his desk and his mind should be left clear to deal with major items of policy. The Bains proposal was that the traditional legal and administrative duties of the Clerk be transferred to a new type of chief officer – the Secretary of a local authority. Not all councils have adopted the view that their Chief Executive should be spared departmental cares. It can be argued that if the top administrator sits apart in semi-isolation he will find it more difficult to keep in touch with contemporary problems; that without a department to support him he lacks eyes and ears to tell him what is taking place throughout the whole organisation. A remedy for the threatened isolation is to give the Chief Executive a small personal staff and research staff. Of course, such appointments involve added expense and there is still a tendency in local government to think of research as an unnecessary luxury. The real danger of a central research unit is that it may be given work better undertaken within the specialised departments.

The Bains theory was that the Chief Executive would promote co-ordinated decision-making through the assistance of a management team, a kind of Cabinet of officials, formed from the more important chief officers. The existence of the management team should be formally recognised by the council. Inter-disciplinary teams of officials should be formed to advise the various committees. This suggestion and the parallel recommendation that committee responsibilities should not be allocated on a simple functional basis were both designed to check the tendency for local administration to develop separate departmental empires and loyalties based on the provision of particular services. To put the matter in the more formal language used in the report – there should be a corporate approach to management rather than a departmental approach.

It may be useful to bring these ideas together, as far as possible in diagrammatic form. On the next page is illustrated the Bains model for the committee structure of a non-metropolitan county. The crucial issue is the relationship between the Policy Committee and the other main committees. It appears that the task of the Policy Committee was to be less than control. It was to advise the council on the merits of programmes submitted by other committees: the Bains scheme mentions concurrent reports to the full council. The idea was that the Policy Committee should co-ordinate rather than command. The practice, no doubt, will vary from place to place. Where political organisation is strong a Policy Committee must reflect the views of (the leaders of) the majority group, and it can be assumed that other committees and sub-committees will adjust themselves to carry out the political programme of the majority party.

Alternative patterns for departmental structure were suggested by the Bains Report. The simpler arrangement was that each chief officer would organise his own department and be independent, subject to co-ordination by the management team – of which he might not be a member – and by the Chief Executive and, of course, the ultimate control of the local council. The other pattern grouped certain departments together under a Director. One such grouping could be education, libraries and amenities and recreation. Another could be planning, transport, engineering, architecture, valuation and estates all placed under a Director of Technical Services. Multi-departmental directors would belong to the management

PROPOSED COMMITTEE STRUCTURE:
NON-METROPOLITAN COUNTY

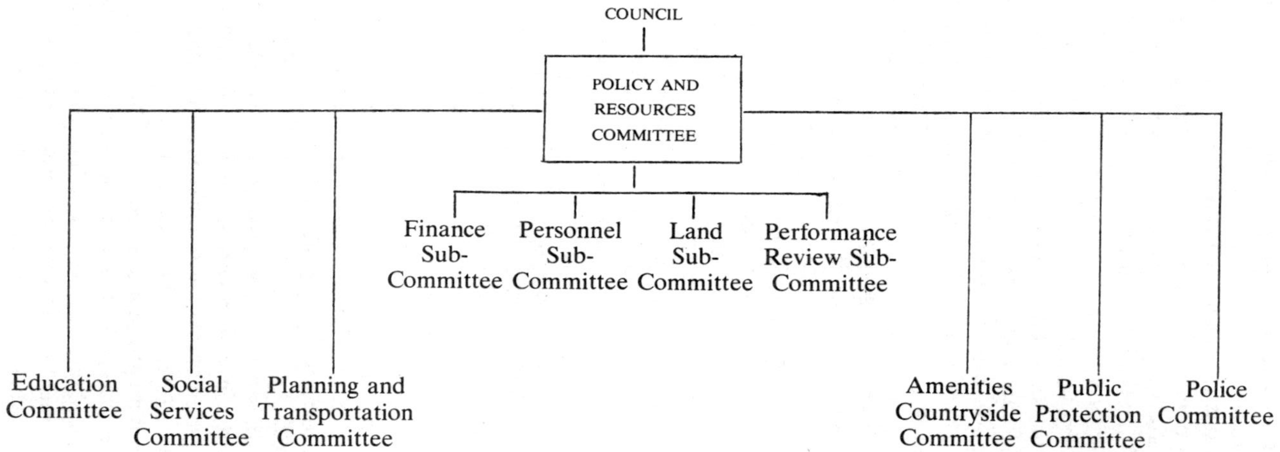

COUNCIL

POLICY AND
RESOURCES
COMMITTEE

Education
Committee

Social
Services
Committee

Planning and
Transportation
Committee

Finance
Sub-
Committee

Personnel
Sub-
Committee

Land
Sub-
Committee

Performance
Review Sub-
Committee

Amenities
Countryside
Committee

Public
Protection
Committee

Police
Committee

team but would be subject to co-ordination in the same way as other chief officers.

Models based on similar principles can easily be constructed for non-metropolitan districts and the metropolitan authorities. The Bains Report suggested that the smaller districts might have as few as three functional committees dealing with housing, development and leisure services, and environmental health. In such places all chief officers would belong to the management team.

The Bains Report was highly influential partly because it reflected concepts already adopted by many of the more vigorous and forward looking authorities. After the 1974 reorganisation almost all authorities had a Chief Executive, a management team and a Policy and Resources Committee all with terms of reference based on the Bains philosophy. A remarkable degree of uniformity of organisation was achieved which recognised the basic need for co-ordination of operations. However, the Bains recommendation to establish a performance review sub-committee has been adopted by only a minority of authorities. The majority may feel that the task of performance review may be left to the committees dealing with each separate function. Alternatively, the concept may be too uncomfortable to be accepted. Performance review suggests that an inspector will call to check on progress. If the report is unsatisfactory, then who or what is to blame? If the administration of a project has been unsatisfactory, probably officials are at fault. But if the difficulties relate to finance or unexpected policy implications, then the councillors are open to challenge. To create a sub-committee whose task is to discover how far things have gone to plan is to create an opportunity for criticism, one that could well be used for political advantage. So local authorities have tended to evade the Bains invitation to self-investigation. It must be recognised that this evasion does imply an unwillingness to accept the full vigour of the idea of corporate management which requires the establishment of objectives, followed by scrutiny of performance and followed again, where necessary, by adjustments to a programme in the light of experience.

One criticism of the Bains Report is that it ignored the element of party politics in local government. But would it have been appropriate for a group of officials to make recommendations about political organisation? Again, the style of local political conventions is so diverse that an attempt to prescribe a single mould for them would be both unrealistic and undesirable. A great advantage of the Bains proposals is that they were not too precise and could readily be adapted to meet local situations. But the idea of corporate management may work less smoothly in a period of contraction. In an optimistic atmosphere of expanding horizons, separate departments may be happy to come together to plan the future. If the dominant issue is how to make economy cuts, then officials may look to their own committees for protection. As for the councillors, the question is, how are they willing to see their own role? How many are able to think in terms of sophisticated management concepts like objectives, priorities and programme review? One fears that many councillors are baffled by the technicalities of local finance. They may be frustrated by the slow pace of change in local administration; they may feel hemmed in by what has been decided in the past and often decided by central government rather than the local council. The Maud Committee demonstrated that many councillors were more comfortable with the relatively trivial agenda items because they were easier to comprehend.

Some councillors resent the concept of corporate management because it causes additional and unnecessary expense. Also they feel it increases the influence of officials to an undesirable extent. There can be no doubt that if senior staff work together to produce co-ordinated advice, then that advice will be very persuasive. The less able councillors may come to feel that the bureaucracy are controlling policy. In practice, the influence of the management team will vary in its extent. Where a council has a party political majority, and the majority group has effective leaders, then council opinion will remain powerful. Some chief officers feel that corporate management undermines their personal responsibility for their own department. Management teams work differently; many aspects of their activities are unclear. What is the relationship between the Chief Executive and the other members of a management team? Is the Chief Executive the equivalent of a President of the United States in that he can overrule all the advisers in his Cabinet? Or is the Chief Executive to act more in the mould of a British Prime Minister who, while having great influence, can ultimately be overborne by his Cabinet colleagues? What is the strength of a decision by a management team? Is it collectively binding on the members or can they go away and give confidential advice, say, to their committee chairman, in opposition to the corporate decision? Can the interests of a department not directly or permanently represented on the management team be fully safeguarded? If a chief officer presents proposals or information to the management team will his committee chairman know what he is doing? All these items are potentially delicate issues. There is no uniformity in the manner in which they are resolved. In many councils a lot of the questions are never asked, at least in public.

MODERN TECHNIQUES OF MANAGEMENT

There is a third broad aspect of the quest for efficiency in local government which covers the various techniques that have been developed to improve and monitor the output of office and outdoor staff. They involve investigation combined with an element of numerical analysis. Processes of this type can also be used to organise information to aid decision-making of the kind discussed above. The following paragraphs give an outline of these methods, their uses and their limitations.

Comparative statistics provide a simple and fairly obvious method of seeking to aid efficiency. If Council A spends more per head on administration than Council B, then perhaps it is wasteful. If a local education authority has a significantly more generous staff/pupil ratio than other authorities, then perhaps it is extravagant. The figures can be used to support an argument that expenditure should be cut back. Yet such analysis is open to a variety of objections. It may be claimed that like is not being compared with like. A scattered rural population is more expensive to administer than the same number of people gathered into a compact urban community. A seaside resort with many elderly residents will need more social services than a population of similar size but with a normal age distribution. Again, the argument about extravagance can be turned inside out. Parents in areas where the staff/pupil ratio is poorer can claim that their authority should improve standards and spend more. The 'league tables' that show the expenditure per head of each authority on each service leave both the high spenders and the low spenders open to different types of criticism. Thus the difficulty when using statistics is to separate indicators of cost-effectiveness from the consequences of deliberate policy about quality of provision.

Operational research involves the study of routine tasks by specialists skilled in scientific observation who are usually expert statisticians. The idea is that an essentially mathematical investigation can provide valuable information that will act as a guide towards making the best possible decisions. A few examples will help to demonstrate the kind of problems that can be submitted to this type of examination. Invoices are normally checked to ensure that they are correct both in terms of arithmetic and as a record of goods received. But checking invoices costs money. How far would it be economical in any office to save the cost of checking and bear the risk of loss through inaccuracies going undetected? In any store, whether of materials needed in construction or in a store of office materials, the problem arises of how large an order to place for any item in regular demand. Infrequent ordering of large quantities saves time and trouble and may offer discounts for purchase in bulk, but large stocks demand larger storage space and involve spending money before it is absolutely necessary. What point on the scale between infrequent big orders and many small orders will give the best results? A proportion of outside staff employed on refuse collection is always absent from work for sickness or other reasons; if a refuse collection service is to be constantly regular some surplus labour will have to be employed to make up for the absentees. How much surplus labour is necessary to give a guarantee of regular collection? These are the type of questions to which operational research is applied. It is not possible, of course, within the confines of a short book on local government to explain the mathematical techniques which are used in the solution of such problems.

This sort of research is not an infallible magic that can always lead the way to the best possible decision. Major decisions usually involve judgements which may be of a political nature or simply raise the issue of how much people are prepared to pay to achieve a certain quality of service. Let us revert to the example of refuse collection. A piece of operational research might show that if 20 per cent more dustmen are employed above the number required if all men were always on duty, then the chances of maintaining regular collection are about 99 per cent. But a council might well take the view that they were prepared to face a higher risk of irregular collection rather than bear the cost of the additional labour involved. Or to revert to the case of invoice-checking, a council might not be willing to reduce standards of internal auditing because of the visitations of the District Auditor. But operational research can provide a firm basis of information on which decisions can be made. Without such impersonal investigation decisions on administrative methods will be made on the basis of hopes, hunches, or traditions, that is, a problem is dealt with in a particular way simply because it was handled like that in the past when, quite possibly, conditions of scale or cost were different.

Cost–benefit analysis is another technique that has been developed to aid decision-making. This is more usually applied to projected future capital developments. If there are alternative schemes for highway development, the more expensive providing for freer, faster and perhaps safer traffic flow, which should be chosen? The idea of cost–benefit analysis, put simply, is to estimate the costs and benefits of alternative plans and to demonstrate their relative advantages. Here again there are substantial difficulties. Any estimate of future benefit must be hypothetical to some degree. Some benefits cannot be quantified or translated into monetary terms, for example, a design for a road or a building may be aesthetically more pleasing than a cheaper design, but one cannot make a scientific estimate of the benefit to be derived from beauty. And when an analysis is completed there remains the basic value judgement of how much we are prepared to contribute now to benefit the next generation. This can be illustrated again in terms of highway development. Given certain expectations of the growth of motor traffic, a relatively modest scheme of highway improvement may be thought adequate to meet the needs of the next decade while a more elaborate scheme would be adequate for a much longer period. Which scheme should be adopted? Cost–benefit analysis cannot answer this problem. It can provide material upon which a more informed judgement can be made in that people can be made aware of the probable consequences of any decision.

This new emphasis on research and quantification as a pre-liminary to the taking of decisions has increased the need to carry out complex calculations with speed and accuracy. The growth of local authority administration also demands that routine office work be mechanised as far as possible. Together these requirements have produced a rapid increase in the use of computers in local government; many large councils have installed their own machine and often arrange to share their use with neighbouring authorities. A computer is a highly sophisticated piece of electronic technology. Only a limited number of specialists understand fully how they work. But it will be necessary for an increasing number of administrators to know what computers can do to help and, indeed, to know how to give instructions to the machines. Hence the very great interest in systems analysis and computer programming. Applications of the new technology are developing steadily: some of their most common uses are for regular payments of all kinds, for example, wages and interest charges, the preparation of election registers, data storage and the analysis of expenditure and income, of costing, and of statistics relating to planning applications, traffic flows, housing lists and education.

The growth of interest among local authorities in management techniques has led them to appoint specialised staff to develop their applications. In addition, with the encouragement of financial help from the central government, a national agency has been formed to give assistance to local councils. This body is LAMSAC, Local Authorities Management Services Advisory Committee; it issues advice to authorities based on detailed research and also provides a confidential consultancy service for individual authorities. Problems dealt with include the desirability of installing a computer, changing an existing computer, or how to introduce job evaluation on incentive bonus schemes. LAMSAC has established groups to investigate some management aspect of every major local function. All this work obtains little publicity. It also faces the obstacles that if improved administrative methods reduce workload then the contentious issue of redundancy emerges. Economies may be achieved by not filling vacancies and be redeployment. But, in a period of high unemployment, there is less labour mobility so there is less possibility of cutting staffing costs painlessly. A major attraction of management studies has been that they promised to reduce expenditure. However, because of understandable trade union pressure, this promise may not always be fully achieved.

The Thatcher government tried to improve the performances of local authorities by instilling some competition into their affairs. Competition is a traditional means of attempting to promote efficiency. However, the scope for it in local government is clearly limited. Public bodies are responsible for the provision of services for the public good; they are not devoted to the profit motive. Public services, for the most part, are not of a kind which permits alternative sources of provision. There can scarcely be a choice of sewers or competition in environmental planning. The main opportunity for competition arises in relation to construction and maintenance work. The Thatcher government is keen to reduce public expenditure, encourage efficiency and assist the private sector of the economy; all these objectives are aided by requiring local authority construction work to be subject to competitive tendering.

Many local authorities have arranged for much of their building work to be carried out by their own permanent staff. This system is known as a direct labour organisation. It removes the need to seek bids from outside contractors but arguably removes the spur of competition. The Local Government, Planning and Land Act 1980 produced a set of rules to which direct labour organisations must conform. Separate financial accounts must be kept; for all jobs above specified cost limits competitive tenders must be sought from private contractors; direct labour organisations are also expected to produce a profit on capital employed, the level of which is fixed by the government. Certain exemptions are permitted from these controls. They do not cover direct labour organisations with less than thirty employees. Nor do they include the maintenance of parks and playing fields. But these controls do provide an important extension to the national rule system that local authorities are required to obey. Further, they are powerfully reinforced by the ability of the government to close down the whole or a part of a direct labour organisation if, after three years, it fails to produce a return on capital similar to that earned by private enterprise. The issue here is not what local councils should do or not do, or how much should be spent: the direct labour controls reduce local discretion about *how* duties shall be done in the course of efficiency.

Meanwhile, there is widespread public belief that local authorities are not as efficient as they could or should be. A management expert based within an organisation may well hesitate to bring forward suggestions that are unpalatable to his colleagues. To have bite, a management review must come from outside. For this reason, the Layfield Committee encouraged the audit service to take a more positive role in promoting efficiency, and there has been a clear response. Reports from the Chief Inspector of Audit now include a variety of suggestions for improving cost-effectiveness. It has been noted that the cost of payment of salaries and wages would be reduced if payment could be made monthly rather than weekly. Warnings have been given about 'pressure selling' by firms and offers of gifts or prizes. Concern has been expressed about the character of incentive bonus schemes and the quality of control over building contracts. Occasionally the comment seems to be directed at central government rather than at local government, for example, the criticism of the complexity of the system of housing subsidies. More work has been done to collect statistics about performance. Authorities whose efficiency falls below the average can be asked for justification. The audit service, supported by comparative information, can face local government officials with a quality of challenge that councillors are not able to produce. Why do you take longer to re-let council houses than other authorities? Why do your dustcarts carry less rubbish each day than those elsewhere? Such questions are useful for they can improve the quality of management. However, some Labour councillors are uneasy about the greater vigour of the audit. The fear is that it could lead to dispute about an issue of policy, for example, over the employment of staff, and that this situation would lead back to the Poplar case where judges had to decide on the reasonableness of the decisions of elected representatives.

Chapter 8

LOCAL GOVERNMENT AND SOCIETY

THE PATTERN OF PRESSURES

It is important to visualise local government in the context of the sum total of its social relationships. This can be assisted by means of a diagram. The chart on the next page is a sort of map which shows how a local authority fits in with the public, the central government, with political parties and other voluntary organisations. It shows the flow of pressure and experience between these parts of the social system – the channels through which demands are made upon a local council, how the council itself may try to exert influence, how the council's services may arouse public reaction and how central government agencies help to supervise local services. Inevitably the diagram involves much simplification. It omits some links which are not immediately significant for the individual local authority. A chart cannot demonstrate the complex relationship within the council organisation between elected members and officers. But it does show the essential circularity of local administration – how people make demands on local authorities and subsequently react to how their demands are met. The chart is also able to distinguish those formal relationships which are enshrined in law. Statutory relationships are indicated by a continuous line and informal ones by a broken line. Most of these links operate on a two-way basis, for example, the local authority associations have an effect on government policy but the government also has an impact on the attitudes of the associations. It may sometimes be a matter of doubt which is having the greater influence on the other. This while local opinion may conceivably take note of the speeches of councillors acting as local opinion leaders, the constitutional position is that the voters choose councillors to represent local opinion.

It should be remembered that the diagram is purely *descriptive*. It does nothing to explain what sort of decision a council will make in any given set of circumstances. This is because it is not possible to quantify pressures or to assess precisely the effect of influences pulling in opposite directions. The diagram is merely an aid to understanding the social situation within which local government must work. In particular it illustrates how various voluntary organisations can have an impact on local administration. The

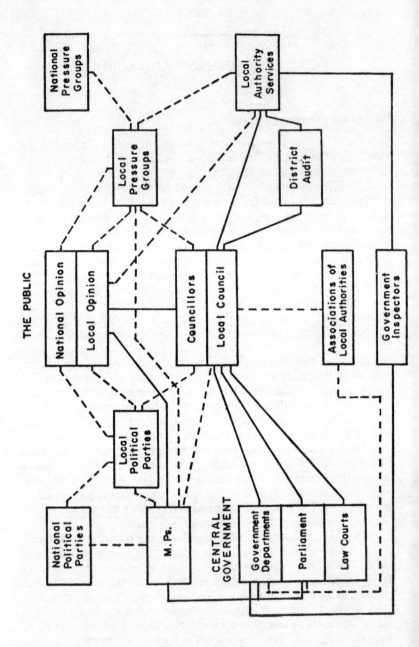

churches are among the most important of these bodies; in the past they had a dominating position in relation to education. The Lord's Day Observance Society may be stung into action if a local authority arranges or permits some activity on a Sunday. Tenants associations are today among the most vigorous local groups and may organise protests if council house rents are increased. And there are a mass of other bodies urging a wide variety of policies on local authorities: progress in education, anti-fluoridation, rural preservation, and so on. The interest of voluntary organisations in local government appears to be growing. They are a peculiarly valuable element in maintaining a spirit of local democracy as they frequently promote causes that cut across the lines of political party policies.

At least two other aspects of the chart demand comment. It shows that the local council decides policy in relation to local services, but it must not be forgotten that the experience of being a member of a local authority and gaining knowledge about local government functions may itself influence members of local councils. A new councillor may think that better standards of service should be provided; after some months on the council he may change his view as he comes to appreciate the financial and other difficulties. Alternatively, a new councillor may be critical of policies he feels to be extravagant; on a fuller acquaintance with the benefits derived from these policies he may come to accept that they are justified. The chart also implies that local experience of local services has an influence on behaviour at elections; if voters are satisfied with the services they will be content to keep the same councillors – otherwise they will seek to make changes. This is the way in which local democracy is supposed to work. In earlier years the theory may have had some connection with practice. Now wherever politics dominates local elections, voters react on party lines according to their views on the performance of the national government. So there may be a big change in the membership and political balance of the local authority, not because of dissatisfaction with the policies or the quality of its administration but because of reactions to government activity.

COMPLAINTS MACHINERY

The growth of public services has provided much wider facilities for everyone. It has also made life more complicated. How are people to know what their rights are? How are they to discover what opportunities are available? How can they feel reasonably certain that their claims and applications have been handled fairly by public officials?

There are two separate problems here. One is an aspect of the general need for wide dissemination of information about local government: this is discussed in the following section. The other problem is to ensure that the administration of public policy is efficient and fair as between individuals. Whether policy itself is fair can be a matter for political judgement and argument, to be decided by public debate and the ballot-box. The task for public administration is to ensure that current policy is effectively and impartially carried out. National government has felt obliged to appoint a Parliamentary Commissioner or Ombudsman to look into complaints. (Strictly speaking, the use of the word Ombudsman is inappropriate. The Scandinavian Ombudsman, on which our system is based, can initiate legal action against defaulting officials; our Parliamentary Commissioner for Administration does not have this power.) The complaints must be about administration – not policy – and must be forwarded to the Commissioner by Members of Parliament. This machinery was an attempt to overcome an evil of mass society, that the shortcomings of bureaucracy may not always be held in check by the traditional means of parliamentary question and debate. But it was also argued that many matters on which the sense of personal grievance may be greatest, concerning planning, housing, education and welfare provisions, come within the ambit of local government rather than national government. If national civil servants are liable to be investigated by an independent official acting in response to a complaint from an aggrieved person, it seems natural that this practice be extended to local authorities.

Local government already suffers so many checks and restraints that it must be asked whether an extra one is needed. The parallel with central government is far from exact. Local authority administration is on a much smaller scale than national administration and the chance that serious mistakes will go uncorrected should be substantially less. At Westminster the Member of Parliament is physically remote from civil servants; he will not know them personally except by rarest chance; he will scarcely if ever meet them. Traditionally, Members have sent in complaints to ministers who will have a political, if not personal, motive for asserting that the administrative processes of their departments are tantamount to perfection. Virtually none of this applies to local government. Councillors know their chief officials and take complaints to them direct. They are, indeed, concerned with the details of administration through their committee work. Do local authorities need Ombudsmen since, in a sense, they have plenty already through the presence of elected representatives? But it is not clear that a councillor can always fill the role of an Ombudsman. If a complaint concerns a decision reached in one of his committees he may be asked to investigate one of his own actions or the consequences thereof. If a councillor does not belong to the relevant committee he may know nothing of the basis on which a decision is made and so is not well placed to make critical inquiries. Further, the time councillors can devote to complaints from the public must be limited by their other commitments. The problem of 'constituency' duties is now more fully recognised. The Bains Report proposed that councillors be provided with secretarial services to help them to carry out this function. Certainly, a councillor should be a first link between an aggrieved individual and local administration – but he may not always provide full protection.

It is vital for democracy that the claims and grievances of citizens be dealt with equitably. This cannot mean that all grievances should be satisfied and all claims accepted. It does require that complaints be reviewed impartially and that where one claim is given preference over another real justification can be found for the decision. Thus if a council house is allocated to Brown rather than to Smith, it must be because Brown has greater need of accommodation, because he has been evicted or is living under more crowded conditions or some similar reason – not because Brown has a friend or relative on the council or because he has bribed an official. In Britain these principles are understood and accepted. There is a tendency to feel that administrative abuses are so rare as not to constitute a problem. While corruption and other patent abuse is infrequent, there are still many cases of administrative errors, failure of communication and lack of understanding. Local government does show concern and respect for individuals and is well placed to set an example for central government in these matters because of the smaller, more intimate scale of its operations. However, the reform of local government structure has now given us fewer but larger units of local administration and fewer councillors. The councillor, like the MP, is becoming divorced from administration. All these factors greatly strengthen the case for local Ombudsmen. But five years of discussion and negotiation were required before positive action was taken. The arguments over the form of the new organisation raised important issues.

The Prime Minister, Harold Wilson, accepted the need for such complaints machinery in a statement to the Commons in July 1969. But what form should this machinery take? JUSTICE (the organisation which popularised the Ombudsman idea in relation to central government) subsequently issued detailed proposals. It suggested that Commissioners of Local Administration should be appointed by the Lord Chancellor; that their salaries should be charged to the

national Exchequer and that they should work though a single
centralised office. Complaints of maladministration would be made
to the Commissioners directly by members of the public. A report on
each investigation would be sent to the person who initiated the
complaint and to the local authority concerned: an Annual Report of
the work of the Local Administration Commissioners would be
presented to Parliament. It would be for the local authority to decide
what action, if any, to take upon an adverse report from the
Commissioners. The Labour government's own proposals were
somewhat different: the 1970 White Paper *Reform of Local
Government in England* (Cmnd 4276) stressed that the function of
local Ombudsmen would be to help councillors to ensure high
standards of administration. Complaints would be made via councillors and the Commissioners would report to local councils and not to
Parliament. The scheme was to be administered through a body
representative of local government and costs would be met from
local funds. Thus the complaints machinery would be separated
from central government and would not be another facet of central
control.

The scheme now in operation was introduced by the Conservatives through the Local Government Act 1974. It follows in
broad outline the earlier Labour proposals. A complaint need not
necessarily be made through a councillor but it must have been
submitted to the responsible authority which must have had a
reasonable chance to investigate and reply to the complaint.
England is divided up between the Commissioners, each of whom is
responsible for complaints from a particular area. Wales has a
separate Commission. Matters excluded from their attention
embrace the conduct of schools; personnel matters; anything that
took place before 1 April 1974; anything that could be the subject of
appeal to a minister or an administrative tribunal; anything for
which a remedy could be obtained from a court of law; anything
connected with the commercial activities of a local authority or with
criminal investigations. The Commissions report on the pattern of
their work to national bodies representing local authorities. Investigations into complaints are held in private. Reports on each case
are to be made to the parties concerned; these reports mention no
names of individuals, but must be available for public inspection.
Where a grievance is found to be justified it is for the local authority
to decide what remedies should be offered. Any remedy should be
notified to the Commissioner who, if not satisfied, could issue a
further report. Thus the Commission has no power over the local
council: the essence of this safeguard is impartial investigation
followed by publicity. But a council that does not respond to

criticism by a Local Commissioner could expect a considerable public outcry.

This machinery creates fresh problems. What limits should be placed on matters to be investigated? The Local Commissioners are to inquire, not into policy, but into maladministration. But what exactly is maladministration? One answer is the so-called Crossman catalogue produced by Mr Crossman when introducing to the House of Commons the legislation which authorised the establishment of the national Ombudsman. The catalogue is bias, neglect, inattention, delay, incompetence, ineptitude, perversity, turpitude, arbitrariness. Put more simply, maladministration would seem to cover any situation in which a local official's action has been improper or seriously inadequate. But maladministration does not include the exercise of discretion. For example, if a local authority is empowered to give or to withhold some benefit, a disappointed applicant cannot claim maladministration unless he can demonstrate some fault in the way in which the decision was made.

Local government officers may be worried lest unjustified complaints damage the reputation and career prospects of an innocent party. Will allegations be made by cranks or embittered and malicious people? This possibility is more serious in local government than in central government for the Civil Service is remote and anonymous. Anyone who alleges maladministration against the Civil Service will only rarely know which official is responsible. A local complaint is more likely to have a personal element. The first safeguard for the local official is the law of defamation. A councillor who forwards a complaint to a Local Commissioner and any report by the Commissioner are both privileged, that is, they cannot be the subject of a libel action. But this protection does not extend to whoever makes the initial complaint. Another safeguard is that Local Commissioners will be fully aware that allegations that come to them may be wholly ill-founded and malevolent. Even so the procedure followed by the Commissioners is open to objection. Statements made by a complainant about an official are not subject to cross-examination by that official or his legal representative. Privacy at inquiries is not the best guarantee that truth will emerge. Officials are not named in the reports of Commissioners but, inevitably, when someone is criticised many people within the local authority will know who is involved.

Another difficulty is that to satisfy the findings of the Commissioners may cost money. This is not simply a matter of paying compensation to an individual who has suffered injustice. Reports from the LCA have criticised delay in repairing a council house suffering from damp; failure to publicise planning applications;

failure to prevent the obstruction of footpaths; delay in forcing a private landlord to repair his property. Quicker and more efficient exercise of these duties would cost money. Thus pressure from the LCA can conflict with the government's desire to curb expenditure.

Only a tiny fraction of complaints result in a finding of mal-administration. Many grievances are outside the jurisdiction of the LCA as they fall within the excluded categories noted above; in other cases there is no evidence of maladministration; in a few instances the complaint is withdrawn as a result of informal discussions with the local authority. Planning, housing and educa-tion are the subjects that stimulate most concern. There were relatively few complaints about social services which may be a reflection of the relative inability of the clients or consumers to formulate their dissatisfaction. To present effectively a case against a public authority requires literary or verbal skills that not everyone possesses. As noted above, the Commissioners cannot force a local council to offer a remedy where a complaint is found to be justified. However, in the great majority of such cases local councils have taken steps to minimise the grievance. Occasionally, to remedy maladministration would be to cause injustice to someone else. Where planning permission has been given after inadequate scrutiny of the consequences of the proposed development, it would be unreasonable to require the demolition of building carried out with the consent of the local authority. A major shortcoming of the local Ombudsman system is that anyone who secures a finding of maladministration cannot, as a result, seek damages through a county court action. It is arguable that this rule should be altered. A council may offer an *ex gratia* payment as a recompense, but that is inadequate protection. Meanwhile, the administrative competence of the Local Commissioners is open to challenge: the average time taken to complete an investigation is eight months. Surely that is excessive.

PUBLIC PARTICIPATION AND ACCOUNTABILITY

It is commonplace that we live in a mass society. All major units of social organisation, with the family as the main exception, tend to increase in size. Employers are fewer in number and operate on a larger scale; trade unions are fewer and larger; towns, schools, hospitals, even universities, get bigger. Government departments and local authorities also grow larger. Taken together, all this must have a great psychological impact on the individual. There can be a tendency to feel lost in the crowd, to experience a sense of responsibility for one's own actions. In a word, a dangerous possibility can develop – some would say has developed – for the individual to become alienated from society as a whole. The public support given to youth organisations and other cultural, social and recreational activities is in some measure a recognition of this danger and an attempt to counteract it.

Local government, as the smallest and most approachable unit in our system of public administration, should be able to play a major role in breaking down the invisible barriers between the individual and society. It is easier to make an impact on local decisions than it is to affect national decisions. An essential aspect of the deterrent which is inherent in the Ombudsman concept is the publicity which will accompany the ultimate report on any case. Publicity could have a greater impact in a local context than it has on Civil Service administration. It could help to lessen the widespread indifference to local government. This apathy was fully demonstrated by the research undertaken by the Government Social Survey for the Maud Committee. Over a quarter of those interviewed by the Survey were unable to name *any* service provided by their borough or district council: in county areas, the position was worse as nearly half the interviewees apparently knew nothing of the county's services. People in London boroughs and rural districts were the worst informed: in the metropolis men and women are lost in the mass society and in the countryside the county council is not so much impersonal as remote. Under one-fifth of those interviewed by the Social Survey remembered having approached a councillor for advice. This picture of indifference is not surprising. Life is short and the potential range of human endeavour and interest is vast. It is not unreasonable to feel that there are other and better things to do than to concern oneself with the problems of local government. Apathy can be a measure of contentment. If people are satisfied with social conditions why should they bother about them?

But apathy may be caused by alienation and ignorance rather than contentment. The nature of possible improvements may be unknown; when produced they may be warmly appreciated although not widely demanded in advance. If local government is to flourish it must take some trouble to educate those of the public willing to listen. Why not circulate to all households after each election the names and addresses of council members, together with a note of their committee assignments? Anyone who calls in at a council office in search of this information will not always find it is easy to obtain. Under the 1972 Act press and public have a right to attend council and committee meetings unless excluded on a specific occasion. There are personal matters relating to staff and financial details of land and property transactions, which should be kept confidential. Access to meetings, however, is not enough. Attempts should be made to explain the major decisions facing a council to the public at large, possibly by issuing local White Papers on the analogy of government White Papers. Of course, where an issue becomes political it is often better tactics to reach a decision quickly rather than stimulate public argument. Local and regional radio and television stations could do more to provoke interest in council activities. Yet councillors and local government officers often treat the mass communications media with reserve. The press, in particular, are sometimes accused of inadequate and inaccurate reporting or of seeking out trivial but apparently sensational news items. Councillors are sensitive about publicity. Perhaps this is due to a desire to avoid controversy; perhaps it is because misleading information can easily create embarrassment for them and may cause needless anxiety for some members of the public.

Some authorities have appointed public relations officers. But public relations work can raise delicate issues. If a council is divided on party lines, a public relations officer who secures publicity for council policy can be accused of implicitly supporting the policy of the majority group. The challenge may be most difficult to avoid in relation to the exposition of plans for the future. Should public funds be spent on the dissemination of controversial matter? Some such spending is justified otherwise the public cannot know the details of the controversy – and many burning local issues depend not on general principles but their detailed application.

The Skeffington Report, *People and Planning*, issued in 1969 urged that local planners should do more to take the public into their confidence. Meetings and exhibitions should be held at an early stage of any major planning exercise at which comments and suggestions would be invited from organised groups and individual members of the public. Subsequent meetings should explain the final form of the planning proposals. There is no doubt that local bodies such as Chambers of Trade, residents' associations and amenity associations can play a useful role in this kind of process. Whether the average man in the street can make an impact on the complex and professionalised task of planning is dubious. How far is it meaningful to think of individual participation in local government? A parent can play a useful and vigorous part in a parent-teacher association that is raising money to build a swimming-pool. But this is merely to assist with others in the implementation of accepted policy. To 'participate' alone to try and influence policy is likely to be unsuccessful and frustrating. It is inevitable that participation arrangements always have something of a public relations flavour: if the planners encourage participation then people may be less unwilling to accept the consequences of planning.

More recently there has been doubt about the value of participation schemes. They are expensive and provide an easy target for economy cuts. Their public relations effect is open to challenge; the consequence may be to stir hostility rather than to secure acceptance. In terms of numbers the response is often poor. Those who do express a view tend to be the more articulate members of the middle class whose opinions may not be representative. A councillor or an official who dislikes the outcome of a participation exercise can claim it ignores 'the silent majority'.

So the tendency now is to stress accountability in local government. The Layfield Report argued that accountability was needed to improve efficiency in local administration and check wasteful expenditure. The Thatcher government also favoured accountability for similar reasons but with particular emphasis on cutting public expenditure. It believed that if the public were more alert and more fully consulted then local authorities would be stopped from spending so much money. To this end, the Local Government, Planning and Land Act 1980 required councils to provide more public information about their activities. Further legislation proposed in 1981 imposed government limits on rate increases; these limits could be exceeded only if a local referendum gave consent. Thus while the Layfield Committee was concerned with cost-effectiveness, the Conservative government also wanted to change local policies.

At present local councillors are accountable to the voters at periodic elections. They are answerable to the courts if it is claimed that they have broken the law. Accounts of local authorities are subjected to annual audit. Should the district auditor make an adverse report, elected councillors may be summoned to appear before a court and face a threat of surcharge if their actions are deemed to be unreasonable. This is the traditional pattern for securing accountability. Yet is it now widely held to be inadequate. What has gone wrong?

Some of the answer has been given in the preceding pages. Local elections are no longer a judgement on local issues. Voters use the ballot to express their view of the conduct of central government; since the Cabinet is normally unpopular, it follows that its supporters usually lose seats at council elections. With occasional exceptions, the concept of accountability for local administration is entirely absent when voters go to the polls. Certainly one reason for this pattern of behaviour is that many voters are not ratepayers. Before 1945 the local franchise was restricted to ratepayers and their wives or husbands. All electors were directly affected financially by the decisions of local councillors. Now, with universal franchise, the link between voting and paying rates is broken. It is not only that many voters are not ratepayers; many who are liable to pay are excused wholly or partially through the rate rebate system for people with low incomes. The result is that a majority of voters do not feel at all bothered by the expenditure decisions of local authorities.

Another complexity is that about half the total rateable value of properties, and in some areas considerably more than half, is based on commercial and industrial premises. Since 1969 these carried no votes. In a period of recession and falling profits, the world of business becomes increasingly resentful of the rate burden as a basic cost over which it has no influence. It is sometimes claimed that rising rates are a final straw which either forces an enterprise to close or to reduce the scale of its operations, thus adding to unemployment. Such claims may well be exaggerated but they do serve to stress again the absence of any link between paying rates and the right to vote. In the eighteenth century the popular cry was 'No taxation without representation': today in local government we have representation without taxation as well as taxation without representation.

A combination of government grants, local rents and charges and non-domestic rating produces over 90 per cent of local revenue. It follows that the domestic ratepayer has to find but a small proportion of what local councils spend. The principle that those who pay should control is, of course, incompatible with democracy. No one argues that such a system could be applied to local government. Nevertheless, one can see that ministers and senior civil servants may feel that they should be able to exercise fuller control of local spending when the national Exchequer supplies so high a proportion of local revenue. To admit that is not to accept that the attitude of central government is justified but only to agree that it is not wholly surprising. Ministers would like local authorities to be more accountable to ministers, but such a development would be incompatible with local accountability. As it is, ministers have a series of specific means to influence local activities but full formal local accountability rests in theory with the voters and, just occasionally, the courts.

It was also noted above that district audit is regarded as a less powerful force than it was fifty or sixty years ago. Auditors now assume that local councillors should have discretion to decide issues of policy. Auditors intervene to investigate possible fraud or misappropriation of funds but they avoid matters of policy. If councils break the law or incur expense through deliberately breaching a civil contract, then district audit can be expected to report the matter to a court. Beyond that it is uncertain when district audit might intervene. Those who would like to check the scale of local expenditure may wish that district audit took a more robust view of its role. They feel that the relationship between local government and district audit has become too cosy. From this standpoint the accountability of local government to district audit has weakened to the point of disintegration. Mr Heseltime is believed to want to strengthen the scrutiny of audit possibly by introducing new personnel from the accountancy profession into the system. Meanwhile it can be claimed that neither the audit, nor local elections, secure the accountability of local councillors in the manner originally intended.

Those engaged in local government will find these arguments about accountability unrealistic and unjustified, particularly if local experience is compared to that of central government. District elections are held more frequently than those for the House of Commons. Councillors are more in touch with electors than are MPs, because there are far more councillors and they represent smaller constituencies. And local councillors are in charge of local affairs to a far greater extent than MPs can control ministers or civil servants. If there is a problem about accountability in local government then the problem is far more severe in central government. A Cabinet with a firm majority in the Commons is untouchable between general elections. Lord Hailsham, the Conservative Lord Chancellor, has described this system as 'an elective dictatorship'. (The Conservatives were in opposition at that time!) Viewed against this background, there is really little ground for complaint about the responsiveness of local authorities to public opinion.

The contemporary mood also reduces the chance of any major reform of local government in the 1980s. Disenchantment with the results of the 1974 reorganisation has left a weary sense that change is expensive and that its benefits are often overestimated. Greater devolution of powers to Scotland and Wales might have had some repercussions in England but, for the present, the likelihood of devolution has faded. In particular, the crushing defeat in the 1979 referendum of the scheme for a Welsh Assembly, with powers to influence Welsh local administration, must mean that this idea is dead for years to come. In 1978 the Labour government produced plans for Organic Change in local government which were largely concerned with increasing the powers of non-metropolitan districts, especially the nine districts above 200,000 population. They would have the chance to regain responsibility for education and social services. In effect, the largest of the former county boroughs outside the main conurbations were to retrieve much of what they had lost in 1974. As most of them are often controlled by the Labour Party there was a clear political motive behind the suggestion. If implemented the plan would have introduced new complexity into county administration and policy formation. Naturally the Association of County Councils objected strongly. And the return of a Conservative government meant that the Organic Change theme was buried. However, one aspect of the plan survived. The Conservatives favoured the idea that the planning responsibilities of counties and districts should be clarified to prevent delay and expense caused by overlapping: the general effect was to make districts more independent of county influence over development control.

So there is no great excitement or stimulus to be gained from major changes in structure. The economic situation combined with government policy implies cuts in services rather than development. At least for a short time the restrictive policies may increase general concern over local issues. People may well be agitated over losing services they have come to take for granted. Does public opinion favour better services and higher rates, or poorer services and lower rates? No doubt, the pattern of attitudes varies from one area to another. Local debate on this issue has been largely stifled by the tendency for central government to bear a high proportion of the cost of local government and by pressure from ministers to achieve a higher degree of uniformity of local provision.

Whenever there is public agitation about a local issue, the voice of protest often comes either from an *ad hoc* action group or from a ratepayers' association or residents' association, possibly newly created as a result of the irritation. Political parties seem to be left out. Perhaps the parties are not very sensitive to local feeling. Alternatively, the people who are keen to organise protest may prefer to avoid political organisations in order to try and secure wide, all party support for their cause. Local agitation falls broadly into two categories – complaints about the level of the rates and concern about environmental issues. Those who are roused to action by their rate demand are not genuinely concerned with local government; when the inevitability of paying is accepted, the fury of the ratepayer dies away. Environmental questions have a longer impact. People interested in preserving the quality of their sur- roundings will know that this is not a matter for short-term campaigns. Threats of development felt to be unsuitable can arise regularly and provide a series of stimuli that help to sustain interest in an environmental pressure group.

THE CASE FOR LOCAL GOVERNMENT

There remains the question, why is local government needed? Would it be a great loss if the system gently disappeared?

Without doubt, the original reason for creating local government has disappeared. In earlier centuries the Civil Service was much smaller: outside London the employees of the state were sparse. For the most part they were tax-gatherers, concentrated in large towns and ports. The central government simply had not the resources to operate details of local administration. If the poor had to be cared for, if the roads needed repair, if local wrongdoers had to be brought to justice – then the existing local unit of social organisation, the parish, alone could do what was required. Now the situation is wholly changed. The Civil Service has an extensive network of local and regional offices operating codes of regulations passed down from London. There would be little difficulty in extending this pattern to embrace the present tasks of local authorities.

Some political leaders might be happier if things were organised in this way. They would be saved criticism, and perhaps obstruction, from local councillors who do not share their point of view and who, moreover, can also claim a popular mandate. Local elections are often embarrassing to the party in power at Westminster; it would be convenient and pleasant if this irritation were removed. No longer would the chairman of a local authority association be able to tell the Secretary of State for the Environment that while both of them owed their position to public opinion, the local elections had more moral authority because they were more recent.

Centralised administration would have other advantages. It could lead to the abolition of local rates. Other taxes would have to be invented or tax rates increased, but the change could well be popular. Greater uniformity in the level of service provision could minimise arguments about levels of local expenditure. The present 'league tables' showing expenditure per head on different services in different authorities is well designed to promote controversy. Either it can be claimed that a low spending council is miserly and depriving its area of services enjoyed elsewhere or a high spending council can be criticised for waste and extravagance. Obviously arguments about local spending will cease if decisions on spending cease to be local. It may also be that the concept of equality is increasingly popular. The idea that no one should be given advantage over his neighbours, unless a need can be proved, is inimical to local government which implies flexibility and variety of provision.

The contrary of the themes outlined above makes an important part of the case *for* local government. To argue that the popularity of national leaders should be tested more often than at general elections is to make a case for democratic local institutions. To argue that rates should be replaced by other less visibile and therefore less painful, national taxes, is to urge that it is right to try and conceal the cost of benefits provided by the community. To try and stifle controversy about the quality of local services is to assail the basic idea of democratic discussion on which our political culture is based. And the pressure for uniformity and equality can drive out the virtue of experiment. Unless different methods are tried and new prospects explored, there is less prospect of progress. If the whole country has to follow an untried policy at the behest of the central government, there is a possibility of failure and waste; yet now policies must be untried if local variations are not permitted. That is essentially the problem with any innovation in the social security system.

The more that government is centralised, the greater the influence of officials on policy. If fewer people are elected to represent the wishes of their community, those that are chosen can have less impact on the direction of affairs. A vast administrative machine controlled from the capital city may produce the benefits of uniformity and equality; it can also be wasteful and unsympathetic. Officials at a central office cannot have the same quality of information about a local problem as will be available to local citizens. Councillors will have more local knowledge than civil servants: equally, parish councillors will have more local knowledge than planning officials of the district council. The system of public inquiries is an admission that the centre needs to meet those who live in a locality before decisions about its development can properly be made.

Decisions made by a local authority are made by people who, in general, will be affected by the outcome. People care about what happens to them and their neighbours. An edict issued from London will be produced in a wholly different atmosphere. There is, at present, a tendency for Conservative ministers to claim that local authorities can be financially irresponsible; yet if a decision to spend more is reflected immediately in the local rate demand, it is hard to see how such a claim can be justified. The irritation aroused by rates means that a councillor is probably more sensitive to complaints about local taxation than an MP is about national taxation. Were trunk roads and poor relief handed back to local government without conditions, would the consequence be higher local expenditure? No one can be certain but the issues would be more keenly debated than they are today.

It is easy to overestimate the extent to which England and Wales is a homogenous community. Different parts of the country do have different problems and different attitudes. Local authorities can and should respond to these variations. Not all areas are equally prosperous. Unemployment varies considerably between regions. The encouragement of industrial development will seem a much higher priority in some areas than in others. Some councils may be wary of factories but seek to encourage tourism. Problems of educational administration will depend upon the movement of population and those in the social services will reflect the age structure of the population. Social attitudes can also vary over such issues as Sunday observance and toleration of nudity on the beach. These examples show that it is a gross oversimplification to suggest that local authorities of the same type have virtually identical agendas.

Yet the true basis of the case for local government is that it is an essential support for a democratic form of government. Democracy requires that everyone shall be permitted to share in the discussion of public policy and that decisions shall be made by vote in a way in which reflects, however imperfectly, public opinion. The process of choice and discussion is itself educative. It not merely helps to produce better decisions but it also induces wider support and understanding for the system as a whole. Such were the arguments used by the Victorian philosopher John Stuart Mill to urge the value of representative local institutions.

Is this case wholly realistic? Elected councillors may come to understand the responsibilities of power better than other citizens, but the 24,000 councillors on county and district councils are but a small minority of the total community. But to their number must be added ex-councillors. In addition, parish councillors have less executive responsibilities but still appreciate how the system works. Councillors and ex-councillors are among the most politically active members of society; they are opinion-leaders. They cannot fail to be a powerful reinforcement of democracy. It was argued above that local elections are often no longer about local issues. Nevertheless, the council elections provide an annual opportunity to go to the polls and provide a regular reminder, both to politicians and the public, that the basis of authority in a democratic system is popular support.

Further, popular intervention in local government is not simply limited to voting. Public participation in planning is widely invited. The public can attend council and committee meetings. Members of the public have the right to question local authority accounts. Public meetings may be held and petitions circulated to try to influence local decisions. Many of these opportunities are commonly ignored; nevertheless they remain. They provide a valuable outlet whenever irritation builds up.

The Royal Commission on the Constitution carried out a major survey of our system of government and took four years over the task, 1969–73. Its central theme was to consider the extent of possible devolution to Scotland and Wales and the case for any such changes. So the Commission paid great attention to the extent and consequences of centralisation in London. It noted that the United Kingdom is the largest unitary system amongst democratic states. The consequences were not always happy. People living far away from the south-east of England felt that the capital city did not understand their problems and priorities. Distance breeds dissent; partly because it makes communication more difficult. A great merit of democracy is to secure the consent of the governed. But this consent will not be secured if it is felt that the governors are remote, unknowing and uncaring. How far this line of reasoning should produce justification for devolution to Scotland is a subject beyond the remit of this book; the claim that over-centralisation damages consent certainly does reinforce the need for a strong democratic structure of local authorities.

Appendix A

SIZE OF LOCAL AUTHORITIES

(i) London

The Greater London Council serves a population of 6,877,000, a figure which is steadily declining. Its rateable value is approximately £1,900 million. The thirty-two London boroughs vary in size from Croydon with a population of 320,000 down to Kingston-on-Thames with 136,000 people. Rateable values vary from £305 million in the City of Westminster to £27 million at Sutton. The City of London remains a unique authority in terms of its constitution and powers but has only 5,500 residents.

(ii) Metropolitan Counties

County	Population (000s)	Rateable value (£m.)
Greater Manchester	2,648	324
Merseyside	1,532	190
South Yorkshire	1,301	136
Tyne and Wear	1,156	123
West Midlands	2,696	399
West Yorkshire	2,064	209

(iii) Metropolitan Districts

Metropolitan county	Number of districts	Population range (000s)	Rateable value range (£m.)	Largest district (pop.)
Greater Manchester	10	178–479	19–74	Manchester
Merseyside	5	180–520	22–72	Liverpool
South Yorkshire	4	221–544	19–66	Sheffield
Tyne and Wear	5	162–300	16–41	Sunderland
West Midlands	7	198–1,033	28–161	Birmingham
West Yorkshire	5	189–724	16–86	Leeds

(iv) Non-Metropolitan Counties

English county	Population (000s)	Rateable value (£m.)	Number of districts
Avon	924	119	6
Bedfordshire	498	80	4
Berkshire	682	116	6
Buckinghamshire	536	91	5
Cambridgeshire	579	80	6

(iv) Non-Metropolitan Counties – *continued*

English county	Population (000s)	Rateable value (£m.)	Number of districts
Cheshire	926	124	8
Cleveland	569	74	4
Cornwall	417	45	6
Cumbria	470	47	6
Derbyshire	898	98	9
Devon	952	110	10
Dorset	591	82	8
Durham	603	58	8
East Sussex	655	97	7
Essex	1,447	228	14
Gloucestershire	497	62	6
Hampshire	1,459	202	13
Hereford and Worcester	617	80	9
Hertfordshire	952	160	10
Humberside	850	95	9
Isle of Wight	115	13	2
Kent	1,456	177	14
Lancashire	1,370	137	14
Leicestershire	836	110	9
Lincolnshire	533	58	7
Norfolk	686	93	7
Northamptonshire	523	71	7
Northumberland	290	30	6
North Yorkshire	663	74	8
Nottinghamshire	974	119	8
Oxfordshire	542	79	5
Shropshire	369	43	6
Somerset	415	49	5
Staffordshire	1,000	121	9
Suffolk	597	76	7
Surrey	993	169	11
Warwickshire	468	63	5
West Sussex	643	92	7
Wiltshire	516	58	5
Welsh county			
Clwyd	385	39	6
Dyfed	325	31	6
Gwent	436	43	5
Gwynedd	226	22	5
Mid Glamorgan	537	37	6
Powys	107	9	3
South Glamorgan	390	49	2
West Glamorgan	367	36	4

(v) Non-Metropolitan Districts

The non-metropolitan districts in England differ from other authorities in that their boundaries were not defined by the Local Government Act 1972. Instead their boundaries were proposed by the Local Government Boundary Commission in their First Report (Cmnd 5148). The proposals were accepted by the government and incorporated in Orders which received parliamentary approval. The largest district by far is Bristol, population 408,000 and the smallest Radnor, population 20,000.

ALLOCATION OF MAIN FUNCTIONS

Non-Metropolitan Counties	**Non-Metropolitan Districts**
Social Services	
Education and Related Services	Education and Related Services
Education	Museums and Art Galleries (c)
Libraries	
Museums and Art Galleries (c)	
Housing and Town Development	Housing and Town Development
Certain reserve powers, e.g.	Housing
overspill	Town Development
Town Development	
Town and Country Planning and	Town and Country Planning and
Related Matters	Related Matters
Structure Plans	Local Plans (most)
Local Plans (in special cases)	Development Control (most)
Development Control (strategic	Acquisition and Disposal of Land
and reserved decisions)	Clearance of Derelict Land (c)
Acquisition and Disposal of Land	Country Parks (c)
Clearance of Derelict Land (c)	Footpaths and Bridleways
National Parks (subject to	Caravan Sites – provision (c)
existence of boards)	licensing and management
Country Parks (c)	Gipsy Sites – management
Footpaths and Bridleways	Allotments
Commons – registration	
Caravan Sites – provision (c)	
Gipsy Sites – provision	
Smallholdings and Cottage	
Holdings	
Highways and Related Subjects	Highways and Related Subjects
Transport Planning	Highways – can claim powers
Highways	over unclassified roads in urban
Traffic	areas
Parking	Public Transport – operation
Public Transport (co-ordination)	
Road Safety	
Street Lighting	
	Environmental Health
	Food Safety and Hygiene

Control of Communicable
Disease
Control of Office, Shop and
Consumer Protection   Factory Premises
  Weights and Measures
  Food and Drugs
  Trade Descriptions
  Consumer Protection

Other Environmental Services   Other Environmental Services
  Land Drainage   Local Sewers
  Refuse Disposal   Land Drainage
  Health Education (c)   Refuse Collection
    Litter
    Coast Protection
    Clean Air
    Building Regulations
    Street Cleansing
    Nuisances
    Cemeteries and Crematoria
    Markets
    Offensive Trades
    Health Education (c)

Police and Fire
  Police (subject to amalgamation)
  Fire

Recreation and Tourism   Recreation and Tourism
  Swimming Baths (c)   Swimming Baths (c)
  Parks and Open Spaces (c)   Parks and Open Spaces (c)
  Physical Training and   Physical Training and
    Recreation (c)   Recreation (c)
    Publicity for Tourist Attractions

Licensing and Registration   Licensing and Registration
    Functions   Functions
  Births, Deaths and Marriages
  Adoption Societies

Other Services   Other Services
  Entertainments (c)   Entertainments (c)
  Aerodromes (c)   Aerodromes (c)
  Natural Emergencies (c)   Natural Emergencies (c)

c = concurrent functions

This table ignores minor variations which may exist in Wales

Metropolitan Counties	Metropolitan Districts
	Social Services

Education and Related Services
    Museums and Art Galleries (c)
	Education and Related Services
	    Education
	    Libraries
	    Museums and Art Galleries
	        (c)

Housing and Town Development
    Certain reserve powers, e.g.
        overspill
    Town Development
	Housing and Town Development
	    Housing
	    Town Development

Town and Country Planning and
    Related Matters
    Structure Plans
    Local Plans (in special cases)
    Development Control (strategic
        and reserved decisions)
    Acquisition and Disposal of
        Land (c)
    Clearance of Derelict Land (c)
    National Parks (subject to
        existence of boards)
    Country Parks (c)
    Footpaths and Bridleways
    Commons – registration
    Caravan Sites – provision (c)
    Gipsy Sites – provision
    Smallholdings and Cottage
        Holdings
	Town and Country Planning and
	    Related Matters
	    Local Plans (most)
	    Development Control (most)
	    Acquisition and Disposal of
	        Land (c)
	    Clearance of Derelict Land (c)
	    Country Parks (c)
	    Footpaths and Bridleways
	    Commons – management
	    Caravan Sites – provisions (c)
	        licensing and management
	    Gipsy Sites – management

Highways and Related Subjects
    Transport Planning
    Highways
    Traffic
    Parking
    Passenger Transport
    Road Safety
	Highways and Related Subjects
	    Highways – can claim
	        maintenance powers over
	        unclassified roads in urban
	        areas

	Environmental Health
	    Food and Hygiene
	    Control of Communicable
	        Disease
	    Control of Office, Shop and
	        Factory Premises

Consumer Protection
  Weights and Measures
  Food and Drugs
  Trade Descriptions
  Consumer Protection

Other Environmental Services
  Land Drainage
  Refuse Disposal
  Health Education (c)

Other Environmental Services
  Local Sewers
  Land Drainage
  Refuse Collection
  Litter
  Coast Protection
  Clean Air
  Building Regulations
  Nuisances
  Cemeteries and Crematoria
  Markets
  Offensive Trades
  Health Education (c)

Police and Fire
  Police (subject to amalgamation)
  Fire

Recreation and Tourism
  Swimming Baths (c)
  Parks and Open Spaces (c)
  Physical Training and Recreation
    (c)

Recreation and Tourism
  Swimming Baths (c)
  Parks and Open Spaces (c)
  Physical Training and Recreation
    (c)
  Publicity for Tourist
    Attractions

Licensing and Registration
  Functions

Other Services
  Entertainments (c)
  Aerodromes (c)
  Natural Emergencies (c)

Other Services
  Entertainments (c)
  Aerodromes (c)
  Natural Emergencies (c)

c = concurrent functions

FURTHER READING

THE HISTORICAL BACKGROUND

Bryan Keith-Lucas and Peter G. Richards, *A History of Local Government in the Twentieth Century* (Allen & Unwin, 1978).
C. Pearce, *The Machinery of Change in Local Government 1888–1974* (Allen & Unwin, 1980).
J. Redlich and F. W. Hirst, *The History of Local Government in England* edited by B. Keith-Lucas (Macmillan, 1958).
Bruce Wood, *The Process of Local Government Reform 1966–74* (Allen & Unwin, 1976).
Report of the Royal Commission (Chairman, Lord Redcliffe-Maud), Cmnd 4040, 3 vols (HMSO, 1969).

THE BASIS OF THE SYSTEM

W. O. Hart and J. F. Garner, *Local Government and Administration* (Butterworths, 9th edn, 1973).
Peter G. Richards, *The Local Government Act 1972: Problems of Implementation* (Allen & Unwin, 1975).

COUNCILLORS AND POLICY-MAKING

W. Grant, *Independent Local Politics in England and Wales* (Saxon House, 1977).
D. Green, *Power and Party in an English City* (Allen & Unwin, 1980).
K. Newton, *Second City Politics* (OUP, 1976).
Report of the Committee on the *Remuneration of Councillors*, Cmnd 7010 (HMSO, 1977).

CENTRAL–LOCAL RELATIONS

J. A. G. Griffith, *Central Departments and Local Authorities* (Allen & Unwin, 1966).
Report by the Central Policy Review Staff on *Relations between Central Government and Local Authorities* (HMSO, 1977).

PROBLEMS OF PARTICULAR FUNCTIONS

J. B. Cullingworth, *Town and Country Planning in Britain* (Allen & Unwin, 6th edn, 1976).
Maurice Kogan, *Educational Policy Making* (Allen & Unwin, 1975).
D. E. Regan, *Local Government and Education* (Allen & Unwin, 1977).

FINANCE

N. P. Hepworth, *The Finance of Local Government* (Allen & Unwin, 6th edn, 1980).

A. H. Marshall, *Financial Management in Local Government* (Allen & Unwin, 1974).

Report of the Layfield Committee, *Local Government Finance*, Cmnd 6453 (HMSO, 1974).

MANAGEMENT AND STAFFING

R. J. Haynes, *Organisation Theory and Local Government* (Allen & Unwin, 1980).

K. P. Poole, *The Local Government Service in England and Wales* (Allen & Unwin, 1978).

Report of the Maud Committee, *The Management of Local Government* (HMSO, 1967).

Report of the Mallaby Committee, *The Staffing of Local Government* (HMSO, 1967).

Report of the Bains Committee, *The New Local Authorities: Management and Structure* (HMSO, 1972).

LOCAL GOVERNMENT AND SOCIETY

W. Hampton, *Democracy and Community* (OUP, 1970).

Dilys M. Hill, *Democratic Theory and Local Government* (Allen & Unwin, 1974).

N. Lewis and B. Gateshill, *The Commission for Local Administration* (RIPA, 1978).

J. Stanyer, *Understanding Local Government* (Fontana, 1976).

INDEX

ad hoc authorities 11, 16–18, 23, 28, 172
agency arrangements 43–5
aldermen 16, 28
Allen Committee 110
Alternatives to Domestic Rates 114
areas *see* boundaries
Association of County Councils (ACC) 55–7, 172
Association of District Councils (ADC) 55
Association of Education Committees (AEC) 57
Association of Metropolitan Authorities (AMA) 55, 57
Association of Municipal Corporations (AMC) 32, 35, 139
associations of local authorities 29, 35, 54–8, 82, 100, 139, 141–2, 144, 159, *Chart* 161
disagreement over reform 29–30, 32
Attorney-General v. Fulham Corporation 119
audit:
district 80, 90, 120, 128–31, 158, 170–1
internal 49, 92
professional 128, 131
Audit Commission 131

Bains Report 27–9, 46, 52, 140, 142, 146–53, 163
Baths and Washhouses Acts (1846–7) 119
Bentham, Jeremy 24, 27
block grant 93, 99–101, 106
Boards of Guardians 15–18, 22, 63–4, 124
Boards of Guardians (Default) Act (1926) 63

Boards of Health 17–19
boroughs 11, 12, 14, 16–17, 21, 27–8, 36–8
creation of 27–8
functions 17–18, 63–5
London *see* London boroughs
Metropolitan (1899–1964) 22–3
Metropolitan (1974) *see* Metropolitan boroughs
see also county boroughs; county districts
borrowing for capital expenditure 46, 69, 102–7
boundaries:
anomalies 17, 19, 27–8
Changes 42–3
London 20–1, 30–1
parish 19–20
see also reform
Boundary Commission for Wales 42–3
broadcasting, local 168

capital expenditure 92–4, 102–7, 133–8, 155–6
central control 11, 16–18, 21–2, 25, 56–8, 68, 71–2, 100–2, 115–38
diagram 151, 159, 173–6
see also circulars, Ministerial; finance, central control over
Central Council of Local Education Authorities (CCLEA) 57
Central Council on Local Government Finance (CCLGF) 57–8
Chadwick, Sir Edwin 17, 25, 124
chairmen:
of committees 47–8, 53–4, 74–6, 79, 83–6, 134, 149, 153
of councils 37–8, 54, 84–6, 90
see also Mayor

Chamberlain, Joseph 20, 84
charter trustees 38
Chartered Institute of Public
    Finance and Accountancy
    105
Chief Executive 87–8, 90, 146,
    148–50, 152–3
Children Act (1948) 64
circulars, Ministerial 33, 52, 90,
    126
City Region, proposal for 32
Civil Defence Act (1948) 124
Clerk of the Council 87–8, 90, 142,
    145–7
    see also Chief Executive
Codes of Practice 126
Commission for Local
    Administration 162–7
committees 45–52
    admission of press 167–8
    admission of public 167–8
    Bains' proposals 149–53
    co-opted members 47, 79–80
    co-ordination of 48–9, 146–7,
        150, chart 151
    criticisms of 50–2
    Maud Committees proposals
        145–8
    meetings of 45–54, 90
    number of 44
    role of 43–4, 48–9, 134, 147–8
    size of 44, 46–7
communities in Wales 36–7, 39,
    70
comparative statistics 154
complaints machinery 161–6
compulsory purchase 119, 122,
    136
computers, use of 156
concurrent powers 44–5, 69–70
Conduct in Local Government,
    Committee on 81–2, 89
Conservative Party:
    complaints machinery and 164
    local government finance and
        100–2, 112–14, 123, 169
    local government reform and
        30–5, 127

Consultative Council on Local
    Government Finance 101, 143
contracts:
    officers' interests and 89
    private interests of councillors
        and 81–2
    Standing Orders 52–4
conurbations 33, 35
    see also London government;
        metropolitan counties;
        metropolitan districts
co-option 47
corruption 80–3, 89
cost-benefit analysis 24, 155–6
council houses, sale of 65, 106, 113,
    123, 132
council meetings:
    admission of press 167–8
    admission of public 167–8
    procedure at 49, 53–4, 90
councillors 29–30, 37, 43–4, 68,
    75–85, 134–5, 148, *chart* 151,
    chart 160, 171, 174–5
    as representatives 39–44, 77–8
    background of 75–7, 80
    calibre of 73, 78
    complaints and 162–5
    effect of reorganisation on 78
    election of 16, 39–41, 160
    number of 76–8
    party politics and 40–1, 73–6
    payment of 78–80, 84–5
    private interests 54, 80–3, 120
    qualifications of 80
county areas 11–12, 14, 19
county boroughs:
    creation of 21, 27–8
    demotion 33–4, 37–8
    functions 28–9, 64–5
    size of 21, 28–9
county councils 20–1, 33, 37–9, 42,
    111
    co-operation with districts 43–5
        see also agency arrangements
    delegation to county districts 28,
        69–70
    functions 21, 28–9, 33, 63–5,
        68–70, 180–3

size of 29, 33–4, 39, 177–8
County Councils Association
   (CCA) 32, 108, 140
   see also Association of County
   Councils
county districts 27–8
courts of law 12, 90, 118–22, 125–6,
   128–30
Crossman, R. H. S. 165
cuts/restraint in public expenditure
   56, 66, 79, 101–2, 112–13, 123,
   127, 136–7, 157, 169

decentralisation 44, 71, 149
default powers 124
delegated legislation *see* Statutory
   Instruments
delegation:
   by one authority to another
      28
   to committees 45–6, 49
   to officers 46, 50–1, 147
Department of the Environment
   32–3
Department of Health and Social
   Security 88, 126–7
departmental structure, Bains'
   proposals 150–2
departments, co-ordination of *see*
   policy, co-ordination
development plans 125
devolution 171, 176
direct labour organisation 157–8
Diseases of Animals Act (1950)
   69
disputes:
   between authorities 126
   between the public and local
      authorities 125, 161–6
   see also enquiries, local
district audit 80, 90, 120, 128–31,
   158, 170–1
districts 33–4, 36–43, 171–2
   borough status 37
   co-operation with counties 43–5
   functions 33, 68–71, 180–3
   size of 33–4, 38–9, 177–9
   Welsh 34, 178

education 28, 32–4, 57, 59, 62–3,
   66–9, 86–8, 93–4, 120–6,
   132–3, 161
   committees 47–8
   development of 19–20, 57, 63
   finance 21, 100, 106, 132–4, 136
   London 31
Education Act (1902) 63
Education Act (1944) 47, 63, 119,
   121, 123–4
election of councillors 16, 39–41, 44,
   73–4, 80, 85, 160
electoral areas 42–3
electricity supply 26, 71
enquiries, local 120, 125, 136
Errington v. Ministry of Health 120
estimates, annual 92

finance 16, 27, 49, 69, 92–114
   central control over 21–2,
      98–107, 110–12, 123, 127,
      133–7
   see also grants, Exchequer
   disparities in resources 93–5,
      109–10
   Green Paper (1977) 112
   internal control of 92
   judicial control over 119–20
Fire Brigades Act (1947) 65
fire services 28, 61, 65, 87–8,
   124–5
franchise, local government 14, 16,
   20, 22, 24–5, 108, 169–70
functions:
   distribution of 28–9, 33, 61–72,
      180–3
   growth of 63–5
   judicial control of 118–22
   power of transfer 68–9

gas supply 26, 71
'general competence' powers
   129–30
general grant 99–100
General Rate Act (1967) 97
Gladstone, W. E. 13, 19
Government Departments:
   administrative control by 115–18

evidence to R. Com. on Local
  Government 33, 67–8
see also central control
grant related expenditure
  assessment (GREA) 101–2
grants:
  Exchequer 21–2, 93–4, 98–102,
    109, 112–13, 127
  general 93, 99–102
  specific 93, 99–100
Greater London Council 36, 55, 59,
  87, 119–20, 177
  see also London

Hadow Committee 145–6
health services 16, 25, 28, 63–4, 71
highways 12–21 *passim*, 28, 44, 65,
  67, 69, 99–100, 123
Home Office 88
hospitals 64, 72, 133
housing 44, 51–2, 64–5, 70, 93,
  102–3, 122, 132
  finance 106, 110–11
Housing Finance Act (1972) 124
Housing (Homeless Persons) Act
  (1977) 44, 64
humanitarianism 25–6

Improvement Commissioners
  14–15, 18
Inner London Education Authority
  31, 36, 69
inquiries, local *see* enquiries, local
inspection by central government
  122, 124–5, 152

Joint Advisory Committee for Local
  Authorities Purchasing
  (JACLAP) 57
joint committees to plan
  reorganisation 54–8
judicial control 12, 89, 115–22,
  125–6, 128–30
justices of the peace 11–14, 15, 16,
  18, 21, 47, 118

Labour Party:
  complaints machinery and 163–4

conflict with councillors 75–6
local government finance and
  99–101, 112–13, 123
local government reform and
  30–1, 34, 54–5
laissez-faire 17, 24, 26
Lands Tribunal 96
Lansbury, George 63
Layfield Committee 100, 110–12,
  114, 130, 134–5, 169
leaders of council parties 83–5
leisure facilities 65–6
libraries 28, 33, 63, 123
loans, raising of 46, 69, 102–7
Local Authorities Conditions of
  Service Advisory Board
  (LACSAB) 57, 144
Local Authorities Management
  Services Advisory Committee
  (LAMSAC) 57, 131, 144,
  156–7
Local Authorities Mutual
  Investment Trust (LAMIT) 57
Local Authority Social Services Act
  (1970) 50, 123
local broadcasting 168
local councils, proposals for 32
Local Government Act (1888) 20–1
Local Government Act (1894) 22
Local Government Act (1929) 63–5
Local Government Act (1933) 81
Local Government Act (1948) 78
Local Government Act (1958) 30–1,
  127
Local Government Act (1966) 59,
  95
Local Government Act (1972) 20,
  27–8, 34–5, 37–9, 42–3, 45–6,
  59–60, 79, 81, 93–5, 128–30,
  167, 179
  distribution of functions under
    61–72, 180–3
Local Government Act (1974) 95,
  99–100, 164
Local Government Board 18
Local Government Boundary
  Commission for England 33,
  42–3, 179

Local Government Examinations
    Board 141–2
Local Government Manpower
    Watch 144
Local Government, Planning and
    Land Act (1980) 45, 59, 79–80,
    84, 100, 106, 127, 157, 169
Local Government Training Board
    (LGTB) 57, 142, 144
local taxation 111–12, 135
    see also rates
London 16–17, 20, 22–3, 26, 30–1,
    36, 39, 59, 63, 65, 67–9, 54–5,
    176–7
London Boroughs 22, 30–1, 36, 39,
    54–5, 59, 111, 128, 177
London County Council 20, 22,
    30–1
London Government Act (1899)
    22
London Government Act (1963) 23,
    31, 59
London Transport Act (1969) 119
Lords Lieutenant 12

magistrates *see* justices of the peace
Mallaby Committee 139–40, 142–3
management board, proposals for
    146–7
management team 150–3
management techniques 154–8
Marshall, Sir Frank 140
mass media 27, 168
Maud Committee on management
    31–2, 46, 48, 78, 129–30,
    139–40, 146–9, 167
mayor(s) 28, 84–6
    abroad 85–6
    borough 37
    town 38
Metropolitan authorities, proposals
    for 30–2
Metropolitan Board of Works 20–1,
    30
Metropolitan boroughs (1974) 36–7
Metropolitan counties 33, 36, 39,
    54–5, 60, 101, 177
    functions 68–9, 182–3

Metropolitan districts 33, 36–7,
    54–5, 101, 111, 177
    functions 68–71, 182–3
Mill, James 23–4
Mill, John Stuart 24–5, 175
Municipal Corporations Act (1835)
    16

NALGO 141
National Assistance Act (1948) 64
National Assistance Board 64
National Association of Local
    Councils 55
National Health Service 72
National Health Service Act (1946)
    64
National Joint Councils 55, 141
nationalisation 71
natural justice, principle of 120
New Towns 39, 179
non-Metropolitan counties *see*
    counties
non-Metropolitan districts *see*
    districts

officers 13, 86–91
    Bains' proposals 149–52
    calibre of 141–2
    central control over 88–9, 124–5,
        140–1
    Commission for Local
        Administration and 164–6
    delegation to 46, 51, 147
    job security of 88–90, 144–5
    party politics and 90–1
    private interests of 54, 89
    professional qualifications of 87,
        89, 140–2, 145–6, 149
    promotion of 88, 141–3
    recruitment of 141–2
    role and influence of 29, 42,
        48–52, 75, 86–91, 134, 145–7,
        149–53
    selection of 88–9, 140
    Standing Orders and 53–4
    statutory 87
    statutory powers 118
    training of 141–4

Ombudsman, for local government
	162–7
operational research 154–5
Organisation and Methods 146

parishes 11, 15, 34, 36–8
	boundaries 19, 42–3
	councils 22–3, 34, 37–8, 40,
		55
	functions of 12–14, 15, 18–20, 22,
		34, 70, 129
	officers 11–14, 87
	town status 38
Parliamentary Commissioner for
	Administration 162
parliamentary control 59, 115–18
party politics 27, 56–7, 73–6, 134,
	152–3, 161, 168
	committees and 47–8
	councillors and 40, 73–6, 83–4
	elections and 40, 73–6
	policy and 41, 49–50, 76, 90–1,
		122
	see also Conservative Party;
		Labour Party
personnel management 140–5
planning *see* town and country
	planning
police 13, 15–16, 20–1, 61, 65, 68–9,
	88, 99–100, 106, 123–5
Police Act (1946) 65
policy, co-ordination of 145–53
politics *see* party politics
'pooled' expenditure 93–4
poor law 12–19 *passim*, 25, 63–4,
	115
Poor Law Amendment Act (1834)
	15, 18, 25
Poor Law Commission 16–17, 63
Poor Relief Act (1723) 15
population, local authority areas 21,
	27–31 *passim*, 33, 38–9, 41–3,
	66–8, 84, 177–9
press 167–8
Private Bills 23, 59–61
Privy Council 37
provincial councils, proposals for
	31–5

public expenditure cuts/restraint 56,
	66, 79, 101–2, 112–13, 123, 127,
	136–7, 157, 169
public health 17–18, 59, 70, 87, 94,
	99, 116
Public Health Act (1848) 17
Public Health Act (1875) 124
Public Health Act (1936) 124
public participation 34, 42, 166–76
public relations 167–9
Public Works Loan Board (PWLB)
	104–5

rateable values 177–8
Rate Support Grant 57, 101
rates 13, 19–21, 29, 70, 92–8, 103,
	111–12, 122, 135, 169–74
	calculation of poundage 97–8,
		109
	cost of collection 108
	criticisms of 108–11
	exemption from 95–7
	future of rating system 113–14,
		133
	incidence of 110
	levying of 17, 42, 46, 59, 70, 95
	liability for 95
	nationalised industries 97
	rebates 94, 98, 170
	supplementary 113–14
	valuation of 42, 71, 95–7, 108,
		111, 113, 129, 170
Rating Act (1966) 98
Rating and Valuation Act (1961)
	97
Redcliffe-Maud, J. P., Baron *see*
	Maud Committee on
	management; Royal Comm. on
	Local Government in England
	(1969); Conduct in Local
	Government, Committee on
reform 27–35, 54–8, 66–7, 71–2,
	171
	Maud Committee's proposals
		129–30, 146–7
	Royal Commission on Local
	Government in England (1969)
		29–32

White Paper (1970) 164
White Paper (1971) 33
refuse disposal 61, 69
regionalism 32
Relief of the Poor Act (1782) 15
Representation of the People Act (1832) 15
Representation of the People Act (1884) 20
representative function of local government 33–4, 37, 40–1, 44, 46–7, 66, 75, 77
representative government, growth of 24–5
research 150
revenue expenditure 92–4, 100–1
Review of Central Government Controls over Local Authorities 127
roads *see* highways
Robinson, D. 79, 84
Royal Commissions:
  Constitution (1973) 32, 176
  Local Government (1929) 145
  Local Government in England (1969) 29–32, 67–8
  Local Government in Greater London (1960) 30–1
  Poor Laws (1834) 15
  Poor Laws and Relief of Distress (1909) 63
  Sanitary Commission (1869) 18
Rural District Councils Association 32, 140
rural districts 18, 22, 28–9, 64–6
see also county districts

salaries *see* wages and salaries
Salisbury, 3rd Marquis of 20
School Boards 19–20, 63
Secretary, office of 149
Seebohm Report 50
Senior, D. 31–2
services *see* functions
sewerage 17–18, 70, 94, 124
Skeffington Report 168–9
Small Dwellings Acquisition Act (1899) 59

social services 33, 44, 61–2, 69–70, 86–7, 106, 124, 126
Social Survey 78, 167
Society of Local Authorities' Chief Executives (SOLACE) 88
staff *see* officers
Standing Orders 52–4
Statute of Highways (1555) 12
statutory basis of local government 53–4, 116–18, 121–2, 128–9
Statutory Instruments 117
Statutory Orders (Special Procedure) Act (1945) 117
surcharge, imposition of 80, 119, 130
systems analysis 155–6

town and country planning 29–30, 44–6, 59, 61–2, 65, 69–71, 116, 122, 125, 168–9, 172
see also enquiries, local
Town and Country Planning Act (1947) 65, 124
Town and Country Planning Act (1962) 124
towns (1974) 36–8, 55
trade unionism 136, 141, 144–5, 157
trading services 26, 62, 65, 129
see also transportation; water supply
Transport Supplementary Grant (TSG) 99–100
transportation 26, 66, 69–70, 99–100, 106, 119–20, 136
Treasurer, office and duties of 87–90
Turnpike Trusts 14–16, 18

Ultra vires 107, 116, 118–20, 128–30
Unemployment Assistance Board 64, 71
unitary authorities, proposals for 31–4
Urban District Councils Association 32, 139
urban districts 18, 22, 28
  functions 28–9, 63–6
  see also county districts

valuation for rating appeals
    procedure 96–7, 108
vestry 12–13
voluntary organisations 66, 159–60,
    168

wages and salaries 55, 88, 135, 140–1
    see also councillors, payment of
Wales 34, 36–7, 39, 68–70, 102, 164,
    171, 174, 176, 178, 181
Local Government Commission
    (1958–66) 31
    see also communities
Walker, P. 32–3
water supply 16–17, 26, 71, 124
Webb, S. and B. 11
Whitley machinery 88–9, 141
Wilson, J. Harold 163